# TEACHER'S PET PUBLICATIONS

PUZZLE PACK
for
The Pigman's Legacy

based on the book by
Paul Zindel

Written by
William T. Collins

© 2005 Teacher's Pet Publications
All Rights Reserved

The materials in this packet are copyrighted
by Teacher's Pet Publications, Inc.

These pages may be duplicated by the purchaser
for use in the purchaser's own classroom.

Copying any of these materials and distributing them
for any other purpose is a violation of the copyright laws.

© 2005 Teacher's Pet Publications, Inc.
www.tpet.com

INTRODUCTION
If you already own the LitPlan for this title, this Puzzle Pack will refresh your Unit Resource Materials and Vocabulary Resource Materials sections plus give you additional materials you can substitute into the tests. If you do not already have a complete LitPlan, these pages will give you some supplemental materials to use with your own plan. There are two main groups of materials: one set for unit words (such as characters' names, symbols, places, etc.) and one set for vocabulary words associated with the book.

WORD LIST
There is a word list for both the unit words and the vocabulary words. These lists show you which words are being used in the materials and the clues or definitions being used for those words. You may want to give students a word list with clues/definitions to help them, or you may want students to only have a word list (without clues/definitions) if you want them to work a little harder. Both are available for duplication. The word lists can also be your "calling key" for the bingo games.

FILL IN THE BLANK AND MATCHING
There are 4 each of the fill in the blank and matching worksheets for both the unit and vocabulary words. These pages can be used either as extra worksheets for students or as objective parts of a unit test. They can be done individually if students need extra help or as a whole class activity to review the material covered.

MAGIC SQUARES
The magic squares not only reinforce the material covered but also work on reasoning and math skills. Many teachers have told us that their students really enjoy doing these!

WORD SEARCH PUZZLES
The word search words go in all directions, as indicated on your answer keys. Two of the word search puzzles have the clues listed rather than the words. This makes the puzzle a little more difficult, but it reinforces the material better. Two word search puzzles have words only for students who find the clue puzzles too difficult.

CROSSWORD PUZZLES
Both unit and vocabulary word sections have 4 crossword puzzles.

BINGO CARDS
There are 32 individual bingo cards for the unit words and 32 individual bingo cards for the vocabulary words. You can use your word list as a "call list," calling the words at random and marking them off of your list as you go, or you could use the flash cards by cutting them apart and drawing the words at random from a hat (or box or whatever). To make a better review, you might ask for the definition and spelling of each word as you call it out–or you could call out the definitions and have students tell you the words they need to look for on the puzzle.

JUGGLE LETTERS
The vocabulary juggle letter game is intended to help students learn the spellings of the words. One sheet has the definitions listed on it as an extra help for students who need it or to reinforce the definitions if you choose to do so.

FLASH CARDS
We've included a set of vocabulary flash cards you can duplicate, cut, and fold for your students. Some teachers make a few sets for general use by the class; others make a set for each student. Some teachers duplicate them for each student and have the students cut & fold their own. You can cut out just the words and put them in a hat, have each student pick out one word and write the definition and a sentence for that word. Students then swap words and papers, with the next student adding a sentence of his own under the last one. You can have students swap as many times as you like. Each time the student will read the sentences written prior to his own and then add a sentence. You can cut out the words and definitions separately and play "I Have; Who Has?" Each student in the room draws a word and definition. The first student says, "I have (the name of the word). Who has the definition?" The student with the definition reads it then says, "I have (the name of the vocabulary word she has). Who has the definition?" The round continues until all words and definitions have been given.

Pigman's Legacy Word List

No.	Word	Clue/Definition
1.	ADOLESCENCE	Period from puberty to maturity
2.	ATLANTIC	The Colonel wanted to go to ____ City.
3.	BARF	Word John uses to be 'throw up'
4.	BORE	How does John refer to his father?
5.	CAFETERIA	Dolly works in the school ____.
6.	CHILDHOOD	A Pigman basically kills a kid's ____.
7.	CONLAN	John's last name
8.	CURSES	What do @#$% and #@#$% represent in John's writing?
9.	DOLLY	Ms. Racinski's first name
10.	FOUR	Dolly and the Colonel won ____ Thousand Dollars.
11.	FUDGE	Gift that John and Lorraine took to the Colonel
12.	GERMAN	Gus is a ____ Shepard.
13.	GLENVILLE	Colonel's real last name
14.	GUS	Phony name originally give by the Colonel
15.	IRS	What government agency does the Colonel fear most?
16.	JOKES	John no longer plays many practical ____.
17.	KEOGH	A retirement plan for the self-employed.
18.	KIDS	How John and Lorraine refer to themselves
19.	LIFE	The only game the Colonel knows is The Game of ____.
20.	MEDALLION	What was the Colonel wearing around his neck?
21.	PAUL	First name of author
22.	PIGNATI	Last name of the original Pigman
23.	POLTERGEIST	A mischievous ghost
24.	PRIEST	Who did the Colonel ask to see before he died?
25.	PROMISE	Name of the introduction to the book, The ____
26.	PSYCHOLOGY	Lorraine reads a lot of books about ____.
27.	RHINESTONE	Dolly wore what kind of earrings?
28.	SERENDIPITY	Faculty of making fortunate discoveries by accident
29.	SPINACH	Kind of cigarettes Lorraine wants John to smoke
30.	STEGOSAURUS	Dinosaur with bony plates on its back
31.	STUDEBAKER	Kind of car owned by the Colonel
32.	SWEDEN	The Colonel was knighted by the King of ____.
33.	TOMB	A mausoleum is a large, stately ____.
34.	YELLOW	Color of the Colonel's car
35.	ZINDEL	Author's last name

Pigman's Legacy Fill In The Blanks 1

1. How does John refer to his father?
2. Period from puberty to maturity
3. How John and Lorraine refer to themselves
4. Gift that John and Lorraine took to the Colonel
5. Ms. Racinski's first name
6. Name of the introduction to the book, The ____
7. Who did the Colonel ask to see before he died?
8. The only game the Colonel knows is The Game of ____.
9. The Colonel was knighted by the King of ____.
10. Gus is a ____ Shepard.
11. A mischievous ghost
12. Author's last name
13. First name of author
14. Faculty of making fortunate discoveries by accident
15. What do @#$% and #@#$% represent in John's writing?
16. A mausoleum is a large, stately ____.
17. The Colonel wanted to go to ____ City.
18. A retirement plan for the self-employed.
19. Last name of the original Pigman
20. Dolly and the Colonel won ____ Thousand Dollars.

Pigman's Legacy Fill In The Blanks 1 Answer Key

BORE	1. How does John refer to his father?
ADOLESCENCE	2. Period from puberty to maturity
KIDS	3. How John and Lorraine refer to themselves
FUDGE	4. Gift that John and Lorraine took to the Colonel
DOLLY	5. Ms. Racinski's first name
PROMISE	6. Name of the introduction to the book, The ____
PRIEST	7. Who did the Colonel ask to see before he died?
LIFE	8. The only game the Colonel knows is The Game of ____.
SWEDEN	9. The Colonel was knighted by the King of ____.
GERMAN	10. Gus is a ____ Shepard.
POLTERGEIST	11. A mischievous ghost
ZINDEL	12. Author's last name
PAUL	13. First name of author
SERENDIPITY	14. Faculty of making fortunate discoveries by accident
CURSES	15. What do @#$% and #@#$% represent in John's writing?
TOMB	16. A mausoleum is a large, stately ____.
ATLANTIC	17. The Colonel wanted to go to ____ City.
KEOGH	18. A retirement plan for the self-employed.
PIGNATI	19. Last name of the original Pigman
FOUR	20. Dolly and the Colonel won ____ Thousand Dollars.

Pigman's Legacy Fill In The Blanks 2

_____
_____
_____
_____
_____
_____
_____
_____
_____
_____
_____
_____
_____
_____
_____
_____
_____
_____
_____
_____

1. Gift that John and Lorraine took to the Colonel
2. Dolly and the Colonel won ____ Thousand Dollars.
3. What do @#$% and #@#$% represent in John's writing?
4. Dinosaur with bony plates on its back
5. The Colonel was knighted by the King of ____.
6. Author's last name
7. First name of author
8. Colonel's real last name
9. Lorraine reads a lot of books about ____.
10. Period from puberty to maturity
11. How does John refer to his father?
12. Kind of cigarettes Lorraine wants John to smoke
13. A Pigman basically kills a kid's ____.
14. Dolly wore what kind of earrings?
15. Faculty of making fortunate discoveries by accident
16. A mausoleum is a large, stately ____.
17. How John and Lorraine refer to themselves
18. John no longer plays many practical ____.
19. Ms. Racinski's first name
20. The Colonel wanted to go to ____ City.

Pigman's Legacy Fill In The Blanks 2 Answer Key

FUDGE	1. Gift that John and Lorraine took to the Colonel
FOUR	2. Dolly and the Colonel won ____ Thousand Dollars.
CURSES	3. What do @#$% and #@#$% represent in John's writing?
STEGOSAURUS	4. Dinosaur with bony plates on its back
SWEDEN	5. The Colonel was knighted by the King of ____.
ZINDEL	6. Author's last name
PAUL	7. First name of author
GLENVILLE	8. Colonel's real last name
PSYCHOLOGY	9. Lorraine reads a lot of books about ____.
ADOLESCENCE	10. Period from puberty to maturity
BORE	11. How does John refer to his father?
SPINACH	12. Kind of cigarettes Lorraine wants John to smoke
CHILDHOOD	13. A Pigman basically kills a kid's ____.
RHINESTONE	14. Dolly wore what kind of earrings?
SERENDIPITY	15. Faculty of making fortunate discoveries by accident
TOMB	16. A mausoleum is a large, stately ____.
KIDS	17. How John and Lorraine refer to themselves
JOKES	18. John no longer plays many practical ____.
DOLLY	19. Ms. Racinski's first name
ATLANTIC	20. The Colonel wanted to go to ____ City.

Pigman's Legacy Fill In The Blanks 3

_____   1. Ms. Racinski's first name

_____   2. Faculty of making fortunate discoveries by accident

_____   3. Period from puberty to maturity

_____   4. Who did the Colonel ask to see before he died?

_____   5. A retirement plan for the self-employed.

_____   6. Phony name originally give by the Colonel

_____   7. Kind of car owned by the Colonel

_____   8. John no longer plays many practical ____.

_____   9. Dolly and the Colonel won ____ Thousand Dollars.

_____   10. Kind of cigarettes Lorraine wants John to smoke

_____   11. Word John uses to be 'throw up'

_____   12. Dolly works in the school ____.

_____   13. What do @#$% and #@#$% represent in John's writing?

_____   14. Dolly wore what kind of earrings?

_____   15. Gus is a ____ Shepard.

_____   16. The only game the Colonel knows is The Game of ____.

_____   17. First name of author

_____   18. What government agency does the Colonel fear most?

_____   19. Color of the Colonel's car

_____   20. The Colonel wanted to go to ____ City.

Pigman's Legacy Fill In The Blanks 3 Answer Key

DOLLY	1. Ms. Racinski's first name
SERENDIPITY	2. Faculty of making fortunate discoveries by accident
ADOLESCENCE	3. Period from puberty to maturity
PRIEST	4. Who did the Colonel ask to see before he died?
KEOGH	5. A retirement plan for the self-employed.
GUS	6. Phony name originally give by the Colonel
STUDEBAKER	7. Kind of car owned by the Colonel
JOKES	8. John no longer plays many practical ____.
FOUR	9. Dolly and the Colonel won ____ Thousand Dollars.
SPINACH	10. Kind of cigarettes Lorraine wants John to smoke
BARF	11. Word John uses to be 'throw up'
CAFETERIA	12. Dolly works in the school ____.
CURSES	13. What do @#$% and #@#$% represent in John's writing?
RHINESTONE	14. Dolly wore what kind of earrings?
GERMAN	15. Gus is a ____ Shepard.
LIFE	16. The only game the Colonel knows is The Game of ____.
PAUL	17. First name of author
IRS	18. What government agency does the Colonel fear most?
YELLOW	19. Color of the Colonel's car
ATLANTIC	20. The Colonel wanted to go to ____ City.

Pigman's Legacy Fill In The Blanks 4

```
_____        1.  Kind of car owned by the Colonel
_____        2.  Colonel's real last name
_____        3.  A mausoleum is a large, stately ____.
_____        4.  The only game the Colonel knows is The Game of ____.
_____        5.  Dolly works in the school ____.
_____        6.  Dolly wore what kind of earrings?
_____        7.  What was the Colonel wearing around his neck?
_____        8.  A retirement plan for the self-employed.
_____        9.  Period from puberty to maturity
_____       10.  Gift that John and Lorraine took to the Colonel
_____       11.  Dinosaur with bony plates on its back
_____       12.  Kind of cigarettes Lorraine wants John to smoke
_____       13.  A Pigman basically kills a kid's ____.
_____       14.  A mischievous ghost
_____       15.  What do @#$% and #@#$% represent in John's writing?
_____       16.  Phony name originally give by the Colonel
_____       17.  First name of author
_____       18.  What government agency does the Colonel fear most?
_____       19.  John's last name
_____       20.  Last name of the original Pigman
```

Pigman's Legacy Fill In The Blanks 4 Answer Key

STUDEBAKER	1. Kind of car owned by the Colonel
GLENVILLE	2. Colonel's real last name
TOMB	3. A mausoleum is a large, stately ____.
LIFE	4. The only game the Colonel knows is The Game of ____.
CAFETERIA	5. Dolly works in the school ____.
RHINESTONE	6. Dolly wore what kind of earrings?
MEDALLION	7. What was the Colonel wearing around his neck?
KEOGH	8. A retirement plan for the self-employed.
ADOLESCENCE	9. Period from puberty to maturity
FUDGE	10. Gift that John and Lorraine took to the Colonel
STEGOSAURUS	11. Dinosaur with bony plates on its back
SPINACH	12. Kind of cigarettes Lorraine wants John to smoke
CHILDHOOD	13. A Pigman basically kills a kid's ____.
POLTERGEIST	14. A mischievous ghost
CURSES	15. What do @#$% and #@#$% represent in John's writing?
GUS	16. Phony name originally give by the Colonel
PAUL	17. First name of author
IRS	18. What government agency does the Colonel fear most?
CONLAN	19. John's last name
PIGNATI	20. Last name of the original Pigman

Pigman's Legacy Matching 1

___ 1. JOKES A. Lorraine reads a lot of books about ____.
___ 2. TOMB B. A retirement plan for the self-employed.
___ 3. CHILDHOOD C. What government agency does the Colonel fear most?
___ 4. CAFETERIA D. Period from puberty to maturity
___ 5. PROMISE E. Kind of cigarettes Lorraine wants John to smoke
___ 6. PSYCHOLOGY F. Name of the introduction to the book, The ____
___ 7. FOUR G. The Colonel was knighted by the King of ____.
___ 8. SPINACH H. The only game the Colonel knows is The Game of ____.
___ 9. CONLAN I. Who did the Colonel ask to see before he died?
___10. SERENDIPITY J. Author's last name
___11. KEOGH K. A mausoleum is a large, stately ____.
___12. ADOLESCENCE L. Dinosaur with bony plates on its back
___13. IRS M. Word John uses to be 'throw up'
___14. FUDGE N. John no longer plays many practical ____.
___15. DOLLY O. What was the Colonel wearing around his neck?
___16. RHINESTONE P. Color of the Colonel's car
___17. STEGOSAURUS Q. Faculty of making fortunate discoveries by accident
___18. BARF R. Ms. Racinski's first name
___19. MEDALLION S. Dolly and the Colonel won ____ Thousand Dollars.
___20. SWEDEN T. Dolly wore what kind of earrings?
___21. GUS U. Gift that John and Lorraine took to the Colonel
___22. YELLOW V. Dolly works in the school ____.
___23. ZINDEL W. A Pigman basically kills a kid's ____.
___24. PRIEST X. John's last name
___25. LIFE Y. Phony name originally give by the Colonel

Pigman's Legacy Matching 1 Answer Key

N - 1. JOKES	A. Lorraine reads a lot of books about ____.
K - 2. TOMB	B. A retirement plan for the self-employed.
W - 3. CHILDHOOD	C. What government agency does the Colonel fear most?
V - 4. CAFETERIA	D. Period from puberty to maturity
F - 5. PROMISE	E. Kind of cigarettes Lorraine wants John to smoke
A - 6. PSYCHOLOGY	F. Name of the introduction to the book, The ____
S - 7. FOUR	G. The Colonel was knighted by the King of ____.
E - 8. SPINACH	H. The only game the Colonel knows is The Game of ____.
X - 9. CONLAN	I. Who did the Colonel ask to see before he died?
Q -10. SERENDIPITY	J. Author's last name
B -11. KEOGH	K. A mausoleum is a large, stately ____.
D -12. ADOLESCENCE	L. Dinosaur with bony plates on its back
C -13. IRS	M. Word John uses to be 'throw up'
U -14. FUDGE	N. John no longer plays many practical ____.
R -15. DOLLY	O. What was the Colonel wearing around his neck?
T -16. RHINESTONE	P. Color of the Colonel's car
L -17. STEGOSAURUS	Q. Faculty of making fortunate discoveries by accident
M -18. BARF	R. Ms. Racinski's first name
O -19. MEDALLION	S. Dolly and the Colonel won ____ Thousand Dollars.
G -20. SWEDEN	T. Dolly wore what kind of earrings?
Y -21. GUS	U. Gift that John and Lorraine took to the Colonel
P -22. YELLOW	V. Dolly works in the school ____.
J -23. ZINDEL	W. A Pigman basically kills a kid's ____.
I -24. PRIEST	X. John's last name
H -25. LIFE	Y. Phony name originally give by the Colonel

Pigman's Legacy Matching 2

___ 1. PRIEST
___ 2. IRS
___ 3. GERMAN
___ 4. STEGOSAURUS
___ 5. TOMB
___ 6. GUS
___ 7. LIFE
___ 8. CURSES
___ 9. CAFETERIA
___ 10. POLTERGEIST
___ 11. FOUR
___ 12. PSYCHOLOGY
___ 13. DOLLY
___ 14. ZINDEL
___ 15. SERENDIPITY
___ 16. ADOLESCENCE
___ 17. JOKES
___ 18. GLENVILLE
___ 19. STUDEBAKER
___ 20. SPINACH
___ 21. KEOGH
___ 22. SWEDEN
___ 23. BARF
___ 24. BORE
___ 25. YELLOW

A. Ms. Racinski's first name
B. Phony name originally give by the Colonel
C. Color of the Colonel's car
D. Colonel's real last name
E. The Colonel was knighted by the King of ____.
F. Gus is a ____ Shepard.
G. Author's last name
H. Period from puberty to maturity
I. Kind of cigarettes Lorraine wants John to smoke
J. Dolly and the Colonel won ____ Thousand Dollars.
K. John no longer plays many practical ____.
L. Word John uses to be 'throw up'
M. A mausoleum is a large, stately ____.
N. A mischievous ghost
O. Dinosaur with bony plates on its back
P. Dolly works in the school ____.
Q. The only game the Colonel knows is The Game of ____.
R. How does John refer to his father?
S. A retirement plan for the self-employed.
T. What do @#$% and #@#$% represent in John's writing?
U. Kind of car owned by the Colonel
V. Who did the Colonel ask to see before he died?
W. Lorraine reads a lot of books about ____.
X. Faculty of making fortunate discoveries by accident
Y. What government agency does the Colonel fear most?

Pigman's Legacy Matching 2 Answer Key

V - 1. PRIEST	A. Ms. Racinski's first name
Y - 2. IRS	B. Phony name originally give by the Colonel
F - 3. GERMAN	C. Color of the Colonel's car
O - 4. STEGOSAURUS	D. Colonel's real last name
M - 5. TOMB	E. The Colonel was knighted by the King of ____.
B - 6. GUS	F. Gus is a ____ Shepard.
Q - 7. LIFE	G. Author's last name
T - 8. CURSES	H. Period from puberty to maturity
P - 9. CAFETERIA	I. Kind of cigarettes Lorraine wants John to smoke
N - 10. POLTERGEIST	J. Dolly and the Colonel won ____ Thousand Dollars.
J - 11. FOUR	K. John no longer plays many practical ____.
W - 12. PSYCHOLOGY	L. Word John uses to be 'throw up'
A - 13. DOLLY	M. A mausoleum is a large, stately ____.
G - 14. ZINDEL	N. A mischievous ghost
X - 15. SERENDIPITY	O. Dinosaur with bony plates on its back
H - 16. ADOLESCENCE	P. Dolly works in the school ____.
K - 17. JOKES	Q. The only game the Colonel knows is The Game of ____.
D - 18. GLENVILLE	R. How does John refer to his father?
U - 19. STUDEBAKER	S. A retirement plan for the self-employed.
I - 20. SPINACH	T. What do @#$% and #@#$% represent in John's writing?
S - 21. KEOGH	U. Kind of car owned by the Colonel
E - 22. SWEDEN	V. Who did the Colonel ask to see before he died?
L - 23. BARF	W. Lorraine reads a lot of books about ____.
R - 24. BORE	X. Faculty of making fortunate discoveries by accident
C - 25. YELLOW	Y. What government agency does the Colonel fear most?

Copyrighted

Pigman's Legacy Matching 3

___ 1. POLTERGEIST   A. Faculty of making fortunate discoveries by accident
___ 2. GLENVILLE   B. A mischievous ghost
___ 3. GUS   C. Author's last name
___ 4. PIGNATI   D. Dinosaur with bony plates on its back
___ 5. PRIEST   E. A Pigman basically kills a kid's ____.
___ 6. CHILDHOOD   F. John's last name
___ 7. CONLAN   G. Phony name originally give by the Colonel
___ 8. ADOLESCENCE   H. What was the Colonel wearing around his neck?
___ 9. SERENDIPITY   I. The Colonel was knighted by the King of ____.
___10. SWEDEN   J. Period from puberty to maturity
___11. JOKES   K. A mausoleum is a large, stately ____.
___12. PSYCHOLOGY   L. What do @#$% and #@#$% represent in John's writing?
___13. STUDEBAKER   M. What government agency does the Colonel fear most?
___14. ZINDEL   N. John no longer plays many practical ____.
___15. CAFETERIA   O. Gift that John and Lorraine took to the Colonel
___16. TOMB   P. Last name of the original Pigman
___17. STEGOSAURUS   Q. Dolly and the Colonel won ____ Thousand Dollars.
___18. IRS   R. First name of author
___19. FUDGE   S. The only game the Colonel knows is The Game of ____.
___20. MEDALLION   T. Who did the Colonel ask to see before he died?
___21. KIDS   U. Colonel's real last name
___22. PAUL   V. Lorraine reads a lot of books about ____.
___23. CURSES   W. Kind of car owned by the Colonel
___24. LIFE   X. Dolly works in the school ____.
___25. FOUR   Y. How John and Lorraine refer to themselves

Pigman's Legacy Matching 3 Answer Key

B - 1. POLTERGEIST	A. Faculty of making fortunate discoveries by accident
U - 2. GLENVILLE	B. A mischievous ghost
G - 3. GUS	C. Author's last name
P - 4. PIGNATI	D. Dinosaur with bony plates on its back
T - 5. PRIEST	E. A Pigman basically kills a kid's ____.
E - 6. CHILDHOOD	F. John's last name
F - 7. CONLAN	G. Phony name originally give by the Colonel
J - 8. ADOLESCENCE	H. What was the Colonel wearing around his neck?
A - 9. SERENDIPITY	I. The Colonel was knighted by the King of ____.
I - 10. SWEDEN	J. Period from puberty to maturity
N - 11. JOKES	K. A mausoleum is a large, stately ____.
V - 12. PSYCHOLOGY	L. What do @#$% and #@#$% represent in John's writing?
W - 13. STUDEBAKER	M. What government agency does the Colonel fear most?
C - 14. ZINDEL	N. John no longer plays many practical ____.
X - 15. CAFETERIA	O. Gift that John and Lorraine took to the Colonel
K - 16. TOMB	P. Last name of the original Pigman
D - 17. STEGOSAURUS	Q. Dolly and the Colonel won ____ Thousand Dollars.
M - 18. IRS	R. First name of author
O - 19. FUDGE	S. The only game the Colonel knows is The Game of ____.
H - 20. MEDALLION	T. Who did the Colonel ask to see before he died?
Y - 21. KIDS	U. Colonel's real last name
R - 22. PAUL	V. Lorraine reads a lot of books about ____.
L - 23. CURSES	W. Kind of car owned by the Colonel
S - 24. LIFE	X. Dolly works in the school ____.
Q - 25. FOUR	Y. How John and Lorraine refer to themselves

Pigman's Legacy Matching 4

___ 1. SWEDEN   A. How does John refer to his father?
___ 2. BARF   B. Faculty of making fortunate discoveries by accident
___ 3. LIFE   C. Last name of the original Pigman
___ 4. ADOLESCENCE   D. Ms. Racinski's first name
___ 5. TOMB   E. Period from puberty to maturity
___ 6. JOKES   F. Colonel's real last name
___ 7. RHINESTONE   G. Who did the Colonel ask to see before he died?
___ 8. CAFETERIA   H. Dolly works in the school ____.
___ 9. KIDS   I. Dolly and the Colonel won ____ Thousand Dollars.
___10. GLENVILLE   J. Name of the introduction to the book, The ____
___11. IRS   K. Kind of cigarettes Lorraine wants John to smoke
___12. BORE   L. The only game the Colonel knows is The Game of ____.
___13. MEDALLION   M. How John and Lorraine refer to themselves
___14. PAUL   N. John's last name
___15. PIGNATI   O. A mausoleum is a large, stately ____.
___16. PRIEST   P. Dolly wore what kind of earrings?
___17. FOUR   Q. What government agency does the Colonel fear most?
___18. GUS   R. The Colonel was knighted by the King of ____.
___19. SERENDIPITY   S. What do @#$% and #@#$% represent in John's writing?
___20. KEOGH   T. Word John uses to be 'throw up'
___21. CONLAN   U. John no longer plays many practical ____.
___22. PROMISE   V. Phony name originally give by the Colonel
___23. DOLLY   W. A retirement plan for the self-employed.
___24. SPINACH   X. What was the Colonel wearing around his neck?
___25. CURSES   Y. First name of author

Pigman's Legacy Matching 4 Answer Key

R - 1. SWEDEN	A. How does John refer to his father?
T - 2. BARF	B. Faculty of making fortunate discoveries by accident
L - 3. LIFE	C. Last name of the original Pigman
E - 4. ADOLESCENCE	D. Ms. Racinski's first name
O - 5. TOMB	E. Period from puberty to maturity
U - 6. JOKES	F. Colonel's real last name
P - 7. RHINESTONE	G. Who did the Colonel ask to see before he died?
H - 8. CAFETERIA	H. Dolly works in the school ____.
M - 9. KIDS	I. Dolly and the Colonel won ____ Thousand Dollars.
F - 10. GLENVILLE	J. Name of the introduction to the book, The ____
Q - 11. IRS	K. Kind of cigarettes Lorraine wants John to smoke
A - 12. BORE	L. The only game the Colonel knows is The Game of ____.
X - 13. MEDALLION	M. How John and Lorraine refer to themselves
Y - 14. PAUL	N. John's last name
C - 15. PIGNATI	O. A mausoleum is a large, stately ____.
G - 16. PRIEST	P. Dolly wore what kind of earrings?
I - 17. FOUR	Q. What government agency does the Colonel fear most?
V - 18. GUS	R. The Colonel was knighted by the King of ____.
B - 19. SERENDIPITY	S. What do @#$% and #@#$% represent in John's writing?
W - 20. KEOGH	T. Word John uses to be 'throw up'
N - 21. CONLAN	U. John no longer plays many practical ____.
J - 22. PROMISE	V. Phony name originally give by the Colonel
D - 23. DOLLY	W. A retirement plan for the self-employed.
K - 24. SPINACH	X. What was the Colonel wearing around his neck?
S - 25. CURSES	Y. First name of author

Pigman's Legacy Magic Squares 1

Match the definition with the vocabulary word. Put your answers in the magic squares below. When your answers are correct, all columns and rows will add to the same number.

A. FUDGE
B. GUS
C. YELLOW
D. TOMB
E. LIFE
F. ATLANTIC
G. PRIEST
H. DOLLY
I. SWEDEN
J. STUDEBAKER
K. MEDALLION
L. PROMISE
M. PAUL
N. CURSES
O. RHINESTONE
P. SERENDIPITY

1. Dolly wore what kind of earrings?
2. A mausoleum is a large, stately ____.
3. Kind of car owned by the Colonel
4. The only game the Colonel knows is The Game of ____.
5. The Colonel was knighted by the King of ____.
6. The Colonel wanted to go to ____ City.
7. Faculty of making fortunate discoveries by accident
8. Color of the Colonel's car
9. Ms. Racinski's first name
10. What was the Colonel wearing around his neck?
11. Gift that John and Lorraine took to the Colonel
12. What do @#$% and #@$% represent in John's writing?
13. Phony name originally give by the Colonel
14. First name of author
15. Who did the Colonel ask to see before he died?
16. Name of the introduction to the book, The ____

A=	B=	C=	D=
E=	F=	G=	H=
I=	J=	K=	L=
M=	N=	O=	P=

Pigman's Legacy Magic Squares 1 Answer Key

Match the definition with the vocabulary word. Put your answers in the magic squares below. When your answers are correct, all columns and rows will add to the same number.

A. FUDGE
B. GUS
C. YELLOW
D. TOMB
E. LIFE
F. ATLANTIC
G. PRIEST
H. DOLLY
I. SWEDEN
J. STUDEBAKER
K. MEDALLION
L. PROMISE
M. PAUL
N. CURSES
O. RHINESTONE
P. SERENDIPITY

1. Dolly wore what kind of earrings?
2. A mausoleum is a large, stately ____.
3. Kind of car owned by the Colonel
4. The only game the Colonel knows is The Game of ____.
5. The Colonel was knighted by the King of ____.
6. The Colonel wanted to go to ____ City.
7. Faculty of making fortunate discoveries by accident
8. Color of the Colonel's car
9. Ms. Racinski's first name
10. What was the Colonel wearing around his neck?
11. Gift that John and Lorraine took to the Colonel
12. What do @#$% and #@#$% represent in John's writing?
13. Phony name originally give by the Colonel
14. First name of author
15. Who did the Colonel ask to see before he died?
16. Name of the introduction to the book, The ____

A=11	B=13	C=8	D=2
E=4	F=6	G=15	H=9
I=5	J=3	K=10	L=16
M=14	N=12	O=1	P=7

Pigman's Legacy Magic Squares 2

Match the definition with the vocabulary word. Put your answers in the magic squares below. When your answers are correct, all columns and rows will add to the same number.

A. BARF
B. SERENDIPITY
C. SWEDEN
D. GUS
E. GERMAN
F. POLTERGEIST
G. CAFETERIA
H. CONLAN
I. MEDALLION
J. LIFE
K. IRS
L. CURSES
M. STEGOSAURUS
N. RHINESTONE
O. DOLLY
P. PAUL

1. Dolly wore what kind of earrings?
2. Dolly works in the school ____.
3. What do @#$% and #@#$% represent in John's writing?
4. Word John uses to be 'throw up'
5. What government agency does the Colonel fear most?
6. Faculty of making fortunate discoveries by accident
7. Dinosaur with bony plates on its back
8. John's last name
9. Gus is a ____ Shepard.
10. First name of author
11. The Colonel was knighted by the King of ____.
12. The only game the Colonel knows is The Game of ____.
13. Phony name originally give by the Colonel
14. What was the Colonel wearing around his neck?
15. A mischievous ghost
16. Ms. Racinski's first name

A=	B=	C=	D=
E=	F=	G=	H=
I=	J=	K=	L=
M=	N=	O=	P=

Pigman's Legacy Magic Squares 2 Answer Key

Match the definition with the vocabulary word. Put your answers in the magic squares below. When your answers are correct, all columns and rows will add to the same number.

A. BARF
B. SERENDIPITY
C. SWEDEN
D. GUS
E. GERMAN
F. POLTERGEIST
G. CAFETERIA
H. CONLAN
I. MEDALLION
J. LIFE
K. IRS
L. CURSES
M. STEGOSAURUS
N. RHINESTONE
O. DOLLY
P. PAUL

1. Dolly wore what kind of earrings?
2. Dolly works in the school ____.
3. What do @#$% and #@$% represent in John's writing?
4. Word John uses to be 'throw up'
5. What government agency does the Colonel fear most?
6. Faculty of making fortunate discoveries by accident
7. Dinosaur with bony plates on its back
8. John's last name
9. Gus is a ____ Shepard.
10. First name of author
11. The Colonel was knighted by the King of ____.
12. The only game the Colonel knows is The Game of ____.
13. Phony name originally give by the Colonel
14. What was the Colonel wearing around his neck?
15. A mischievous ghost
16. Ms. Racinski's first name

A=4	B=6	C=11	D=13
E=9	F=15	G=2	H=8
I=14	J=12	K=5	L=3
M=7	N=1	O=16	P=10

Pigman's Legacy Magic Squares 3

Match the definition with the vocabulary word. Put your answers in the magic squares below. When your answers are correct, all columns and rows will add to the same number.

A. IRS
B. PROMISE
C. KEOGH
D. LIFE
E. BORE
F. GERMAN
G. ADOLESCENCE
H. CURSES
I. SERENDIPITY
J. ATLANTIC
K. POLTERGEIST
L. STUDEBAKER
M. CONLAN
N. YELLOW
O. ZINDEL
P. PRIEST

1. What government agency does the Colonel fear most?
2. Color of the Colonel's car
3. The Colonel wanted to go to ____ City.
4. How does John refer to his father?
5. Period from puberty to maturity
6. Kind of car owned by the Colonel
7. Who did the Colonel ask to see before he died?
8. A retirement plan for the self-employed.
9. Author's last name
10. The only game the Colonel knows is The Game of ____.
11. What do @#$% and #@#$% represent in John's writing?
12. A mischievous ghost
13. Faculty of making fortunate discoveries by accident
14. Gus is a ____ Shepard.
15. Name of the introduction to the book, The ____
16. John's last name

A=	B=	C=	D=
E=	F=	G=	H=
I=	J=	K=	L=
M=	N=	O=	P=

Pigman's Legacy Magic Squares 3 Answer Key

Match the definition with the vocabulary word. Put your answers in the magic squares below. When your answers are correct, all columns and rows will add to the same number.

A. IRS
B. PROMISE
C. KEOGH
D. LIFE
E. BORE
F. GERMAN
G. ADOLESCENCE
H. CURSES
I. SERENDIPITY
J. ATLANTIC
K. POLTERGEIST
L. STUDEBAKER
M. CONLAN
N. YELLOW
O. ZINDEL
P. PRIEST

1. What government agency does the Colonel fear most?
2. Color of the Colonel's car
3. The Colonel wanted to go to ____ City.
4. How does John refer to his father?
5. Period from puberty to maturity
6. Kind of car owned by the Colonel
7. Who did the Colonel ask to see before he died?
8. A retirement plan for the self-employed.
9. Author's last name
10. The only game the Colonel knows is The Game of ____.
11. What do @#$% and #@#$% represent in John's writing?
12. A mischievous ghost
13. Faculty of making fortunate discoveries by accident
14. Gus is a ____ Shepard.
15. Name of the introduction to the book, The ____
16. John's last name

A=1	B=15	C=8	D=10
E=4	F=14	G=5	H=11
I=13	J=3	K=12	L=6
M=16	N=2	O=9	P=7

Pigman's Legacy Magic Squares 4

Match the definition with the vocabulary word. Put your answers in the magic squares below. When your answers are correct, all columns and rows will add to the same number.

A. STUDEBAKER
B. JOKES
C. GERMAN
D. ZINDEL
E. DOLLY
F. ADOLESCENCE
G. FUDGE
H. PAUL
I. IRS
J. PROMISE
K. PRIEST
L. POLTERGEIST
M. LIFE
N. SPINACH
O. BORE
P. SWEDEN

1. Period from puberty to maturity
2. What government agency does the Colonel fear most?
3. How does John refer to his father?
4. Author's last name
5. The only game the Colonel knows is The Game of ____.
6. John no longer plays many practical ____.
7. First name of author
8. Who did the Colonel ask to see before he died?
9. Gus is a ____ Shepard.
10. The Colonel was knighted by the King of ____.
11. Name of the introduction to the book, The ____
12. Ms. Racinski's first name
13. A mischievous ghost
14. Gift that John and Lorraine took to the Colonel
15. Kind of car owned by the Colonel
16. Kind of cigarettes Lorraine wants John to smoke

A=	B=	C=	D=
E=	F=	G=	H=
I=	J=	K=	L=
M=	N=	O=	P=

Pigman's Legacy Magic Squares 4 Answer Key

Match the definition with the vocabulary word. Put your answers in the magic squares below. When your answers are correct, all columns and rows will add to the same number.

A. STUDEBAKER
B. JOKES
C. GERMAN
D. ZINDEL
E. DOLLY
F. ADOLESCENCE
G. FUDGE
H. PAUL
I. IRS
J. PROMISE
K. PRIEST
L. POLTERGEIST
M. LIFE
N. SPINACH
O. BORE
P. SWEDEN

1. Period from puberty to maturity
2. What government agency does the Colonel fear most?
3. How does John refer to his father?
4. Author's last name
5. The only game the Colonel knows is The Game of ____.
6. John no longer plays many practical ____.
7. First name of author
8. Who did the Colonel ask to see before he died?
9. Gus is a ____ Shepard.
10. The Colonel was knighted by the King of ____.
11. Name of the introduction to the book, The ____
12. Ms. Racinski's first name
13. A mischievous ghost
14. Gift that John and Lorraine took to the Colonel
15. Kind of car owned by the Colonel
16. Kind of cigarettes Lorraine wants John to smoke

A=15	B=6	C=9	D=4
E=12	F=1	G=14	H=7
I=2	J=11	K=8	L=13
M=5	N=16	O=3	P=10

Pigman's Legacy Word Search 1

Words are placed backwards, forward, diagonally, up and down. Clues listed below can help you find the words. Circle the hidden vocabulary words in the maze.

```
F X G S H B T R M Y C U R S E S V F C
U B N W G S E P H X A F N F B Y P S L
D A A E O B R K O Q F F G H F J E R X
G R M D E G O F L L E Y U Q Z K I P W
E F R E K A B E D U T S S T O M B R W
S P E N L V D R R I E E S J L K X O S
T A G Q K N V I P C R E R N I K L M J
E U H B I Q T I V B I D K G F L X I A
G L X Z N A D R K R A F L I E P H S D
O J N W N N T S P F H E M Y D I T E O
S P D G E W Y L H S L I Q Q L S S F L
A F I R W J L G A L S S N C K B K T E
U P E F O U R P I N C P Y E D K N V S
R S W S V T X V Q F T L I X S T X M C
U G W H R P N B R T L I N N G T C B E
S G K V Y E G R X O J L C D A F O D N
J X Z K L V G F D C O N L A N C C N C
L C J G C H I L D H O O D T W B H B E
```

A Pigman basically kills a kid's ____. (9)
A mausoleum is a large, stately ____. (4)
A mischievous ghost (11)
A retirement plan for the self-employed. (5)
Author's last name (6)
Colonel's real last name (9)
Color of the Colonel's car (6)
Dinosaur with bony plates on its back (11)
Dolly and the Colonel won ____ Thousand Dollars. (4)
Dolly wore what kind of earrings? (10)
Dolly works in the school ____. (9)
Faculty of making fortunate discoveries by accident (11)
First name of author (4)
Gift that John and Lorraine took to the Colonel (5)
Gus is a ____ Shepard. (6)
How John and Lorraine refer to themselves (4)
How does John refer to his father? (4)
John no longer plays many practical ____. (5)

John's last name (6)
Kind of car owned by the Colonel (10)
Kind of cigarettes Lorraine wants John to smoke (7)
Last name of the original Pigman (7)
Ms. Racinski's first name (5)
Name of the introduction to the book, The ____ (7)
Period from puberty to maturity (11)
Phony name originally give by the Colonel (3)
The Colonel wanted to go to ____ City. (8)
The Colonel was knighted by the King of ____. (6)
The only game the Colonel knows is The Game of ____. (4)
What do @#$% and #@#$% represent in John's writing? (6)
What government agency does the Colonel fear most? (3)
Who did the Colonel ask to see before he died? (6)
Word John uses to be 'throw up' (4)

Pigman's Legacy Word Search 1 Answer Key

Words are placed backwards, forward, diagonally, up and down. Clues listed below can help you find the words. Circle the hidden vocabulary words in the maze.

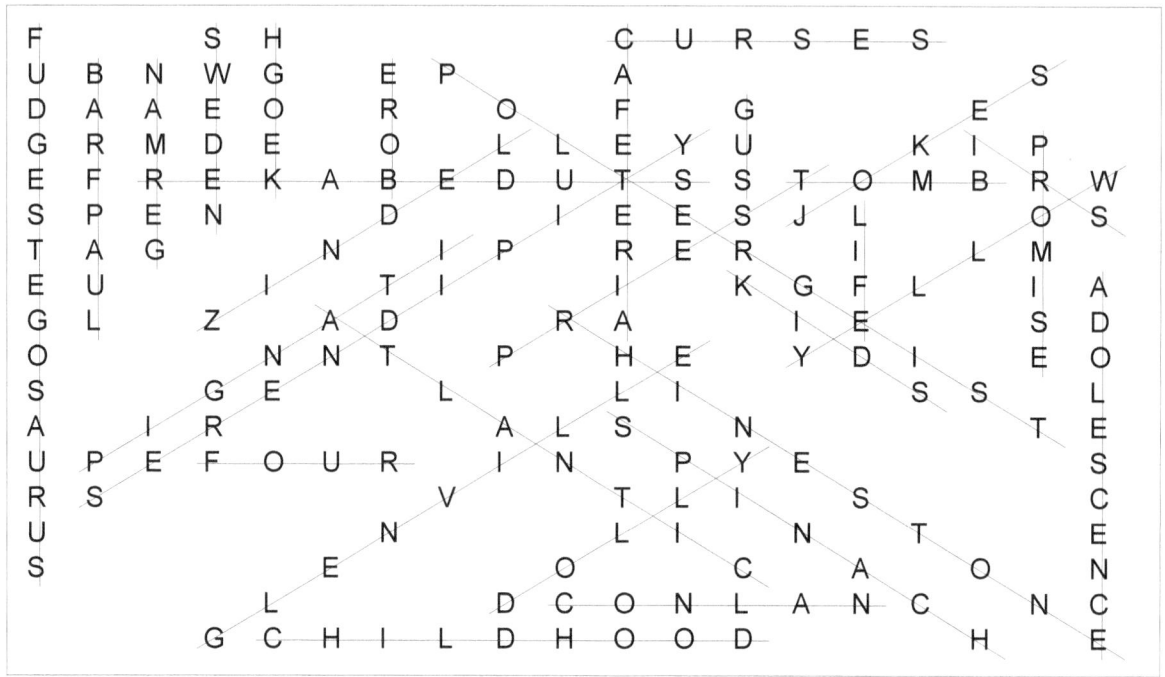

A Pigman basically kills a kid's ____. (9)
A mausoleum is a large, stately ____. (4)
A mischievous ghost (11)
A retirement plan for the self-employed. (5)
Author's last name (6)
Colonel's real last name (9)
Color of the Colonel's car (6)
Dinosaur with bony plates on its back (11)
Dolly and the Colonel won ____ Thousand Dollars. (4)
Dolly wore what kind of earrings? (10)
Dolly works in the school ____. (9)
Faculty of making fortunate discoveries by accident (11)
First name of author (4)
Gift that John and Lorraine took to the Colonel (5)
Gus is a ____ Shepard. (6)
How John and Lorraine refer to themselves (4)
How does John refer to his father? (4)
John no longer plays many practical ____. (5)

John's last name (6)
Kind of car owned by the Colonel (10)
Kind of cigarettes Lorraine wants John to smoke (7)
Last name of the original Pigman (7)
Ms. Racinski's first name (5)
Name of the introduction to the book, The ____ (7)
Period from puberty to maturity (11)
Phony name originally give by the Colonel (3)
The Colonel wanted to go to ____ City. (8)
The Colonel was knighted by the King of ____. (6)
The only game the Colonel knows is The Game of ____. (4)
What do @#$% and #@#$% represent in John's writing? (6)
What government agency does the Colonel fear most? (3)
Who did the Colonel ask to see before he died? (6)
Word John uses to be 'throw up' (4)

Pigman's Legacy Word Search 2

Words are placed backwards, forward, diagonally, up and down. Clues listed below can help you find the words. Circle the hidden vocabulary words in the maze.

```
Y F N A L N O C P R O M I S E J J X N
E X K D M B E N O T S E N I H R V G B
L N C O H T C W X D V D C T P Z D R M
L S M L X Y D P T F Z A B Y S M Q X H
O Y K E H K K G T J W L N P Y L X Q S
W F Z S W K I E R H B L Z X C C R C Y
N X S C P T A C O Y M I F C H F B G V
H X Y E A O T Y D G H O V X O Y O M L
G L E N V I L L E C H N M J L H J U Z
J A G C N Q A T R P H K N L O V A V R
W I S E T G N Z E S H I O F G P B L F
P R J X Z U T S I R V D L U Y B O I H
N E D E W S I P P N G S R D B A R F F
R T K T T E C I R A D E D G H J E E Q
T E W O M S T N I M J E I E H O T F J
P F J M B R J A E R M F L S P K O J H
L A W B H U M C S E I R S P T E Y D T
C C C P L C Q H T G M V H V J S V J R
```

A Pigman basically kills a kid's ____. (9)
A mausoleum is a large, stately ____. (4)
A mischievous ghost (11)
A retirement plan for the self-employed. (5)
Author's last name (6)
Colonel's real last name (9)
Color of the Colonel's car (6)
Dolly and the Colonel won ____ Thousand Dollars. (4)
Dolly wore what kind of earrings? (10)
Dolly works in the school ____. (9)
First name of author (4)
Gift that John and Lorraine took to the Colonel (5)
Gus is a ____ Shepard. (6)
How John and Lorraine refer to themselves (4)
How does John refer to his father? (4)
John no longer plays many practical ____. (5)
John's last name (6)
Kind of cigarettes Lorraine wants John to smoke (7)

Last name of the original Pigman (7)
Lorraine reads a lot of books about ____. (10)
Ms. Racinski's first name (5)
Name of the introduction to the book, The ____ (7)
Period from puberty to maturity (11)
Phony name originally give by the Colonel (3)
The Colonel wanted to go to ____ City. (8)
The Colonel was knighted by the King of ____. (6)
The only game the Colonel knows is The Game of ____. (4)
What do @#$% and #@#$% represent in John's writing? (6)
What government agency does the Colonel fear most? (3)
What was the Colonel wearing around his neck? (9)
Who did the Colonel ask to see before he died? (6)
Word John uses to be 'throw up' (4)

Pigman's Legacy Word Search 2 Answer Key

Words are placed backwards, forward, diagonally, up and down. Clues listed below can help you find the words. Circle the hidden vocabulary words in the maze.

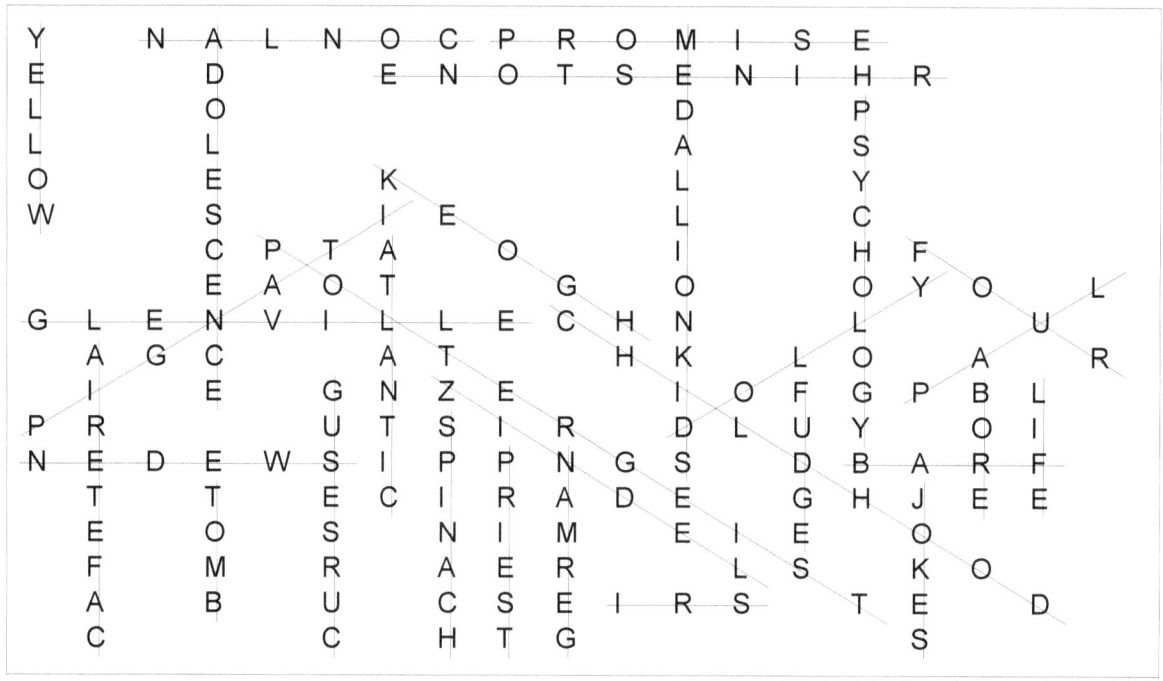

A Pigman basically kills a kid's ____. (9)
A mausoleum is a large, stately ____. (4)
A mischievous ghost (11)
A retirement plan for the self-employed. (5)
Author's last name (6)
Colonel's real last name (9)
Color of the Colonel's car (6)
Dolly and the Colonel won ____ Thousand Dollars. (4)
Dolly wore what kind of earrings? (10)
Dolly works in the school ____. (9)
First name of author (4)
Gift that John and Lorraine took to the Colonel (5)
Gus is a ____ Shepard. (6)
How John and Lorraine refer to themselves (4)
How does John refer to his father? (4)
John no longer plays many practical ____. (5)
John's last name (6)
Kind of cigarettes Lorraine wants John to smoke (7)

Last name of the original Pigman (7)
Lorraine reads a lot of books about ____. (10)
Ms. Racinski's first name (5)
Name of the introduction to the book, The ____ (7)
Period from puberty to maturity (11)
Phony name originally give by the Colonel (3)
The Colonel wanted to go to ____ City. (8)
The Colonel was knighted by the King of ____. (6)
The only game the Colonel knows is The Game of ____. (4)
What do @#$% and #@#$% represent in John's writing? (6)
What government agency does the Colonel fear most? (3)
What was the Colonel wearing around his neck? (9)
Who did the Colonel ask to see before he died? (6)
Word John uses to be 'throw up' (4)

Pigman's Legacy Word Search 3

Words are placed backwards, forward, diagonally, up and down. Words listed below are included in the maze. Circle the hidden vocabulary words in the maze.

```
S T U D E B A K E R A T L A N T I C A R
P Q G J K R S S L C G D O O H D L I H C
G K E C V H B Z L N R Y F V L Q R G E S
J P R J H I Z T I N Z M T G Q E L S J G
H X M K W N Z I V Y D H R P T Z I T V L
M L A N F E X S N Z R S M E R M W B G S
L L N W G S R K E D T N F B O I T I V D
S K C H Q T J T L E E A V R A W E R R H
P S Y C H O L O G Y C L P B O R E S N L
I H S M K N S O D U U N Z W U G F O T E
N F L E W E S V X A S O T O D M I C C P
A W S D D A D S P D S C F U E L Q N P Y
C D R B U W B O K I D S F F L K E O G H
H G M R O P V H L Q T N I A R C G R D L
H O U L H Z P Y C L R L D C S V R L V S
T S L N M F C V L P Y E K E Z W D B E K
T E P I G N A T I L M B L Z G F E S P V
Y G T S I E G R E T L O P K G L R D K W
Q H K K F T B N K G D B T S P U C P E Z
J N R D T R Y P M A V F S F C C Y X F N
```

ADOLESCENCE	FOUR	LIFE	SPINACH
ATLANTIC	FUDGE	MEDALLION	STEGOSAURUS
BARF	GERMAN	PAUL	STUDEBAKER
BORE	GLENVILLE	PIGNATI	SWEDEN
CAFETERIA	GUS	POLTERGEIST	TOMB
CHILDHOOD	IRS	PRIEST	YELLOW
CONLAN	JOKES	PROMISE	ZINDEL
CURSES	KEOGH	PSYCHOLOGY	
DOLLY	KIDS	RHINESTONE	

Pigman's Legacy Word Search 3 Answer Key

Words are placed backwards, forward, diagonally, up and down. Words listed below are included in the maze. Circle the hidden vocabulary words in the maze.

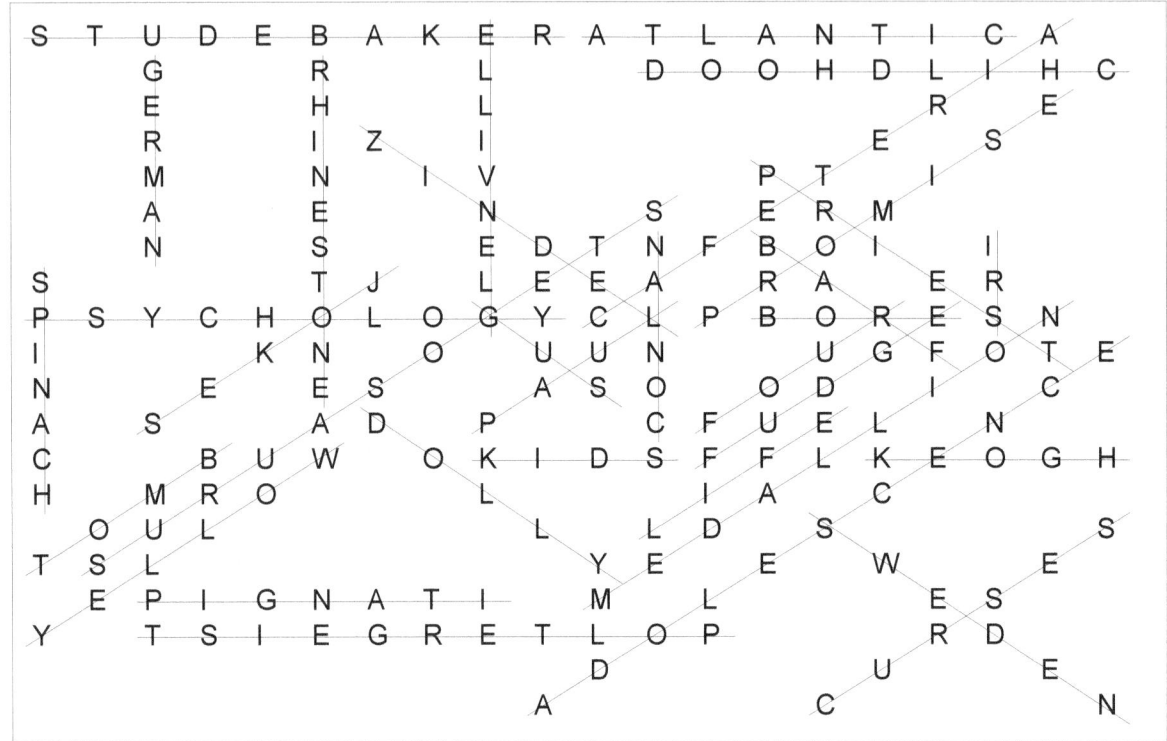

ADOLESCENCE	FOUR	LIFE	SPINACH
ATLANTIC	FUDGE	MEDALLION	STEGOSAURUS
BARF	GERMAN	PAUL	STUDEBAKER
BORE	GLENVILLE	PIGNATI	SWEDEN
CAFETERIA	GUS	POLTERGEIST	TOMB
CHILDHOOD	IRS	PRIEST	YELLOW
CONLAN	JOKES	PROMISE	ZINDEL
CURSES	KEOGH	PSYCHOLOGY	
DOLLY	KIDS	RHINESTONE	

Pigman's Legacy Word Search 4

Words are placed backwards, forward, diagonally, up and down. Words listed below are included in the maze. Circle the hidden vocabulary words in the maze.

```
M Z S C P F P B T T Z F V W C L P K A H
L H E N S G U S E L L I V N E L G I I F
Z D R X W P E S Y W Z M N T B Z H D R M
S S E R Y I I N M C Q E E D H A F S E S
T F N C R J B N N D H R S D E P R P T K
E B D P C O N L A N F O U R A L O F E S
G H I Z M K E J M C C B L U C L U T F M
O L P Y V E D T R Q H F L O T D L B A Z
S C I V R S E G E X G X H E G F L I C Z
A C T F R R W X G W E Q R E D Y L C O P
U L Y T E H S G S C Y G Z W K O R L N N
R T M V B I R T N T E C K Y G W L V F S
U J O B N N M E J I L L U D P H G L F W
S G M M D E C B S K L V W R M G N G Y H
N S P N B S T T K T O M O S S O G C Z X
V C L Z E T Z P N J W M K X T E X M C F
V M X L G O V L Q D I S M J G K S L T N
B D O N J N P V S S C H I L D H O O D R
V D J M Z E M B E A T L A N T I C X Z K
A X D P I G N A T I S T U D E B A K E R
```

ADOLESCENCE	FOUR	LIFE	SERENDIPITY
ATLANTIC	FUDGE	MEDALLION	SPINACH
BARF	GERMAN	PAUL	STEGOSAURUS
BORE	GLENVILLE	PIGNATI	STUDEBAKER
CAFETERIA	GUS	POLTERGEIST	SWEDEN
CHILDHOOD	IRS	PRIEST	TOMB
CONLAN	JOKES	PROMISE	YELLOW
CURSES	KEOGH	PSYCHOLOGY	ZINDEL
DOLLY	KIDS	RHINESTONE	

Pigman's Legacy Word Search 4 Answer Key

Words are placed backwards, forward, diagonally, up and down. Words listed below are included in the maze. Circle the hidden vocabulary words in the maze.

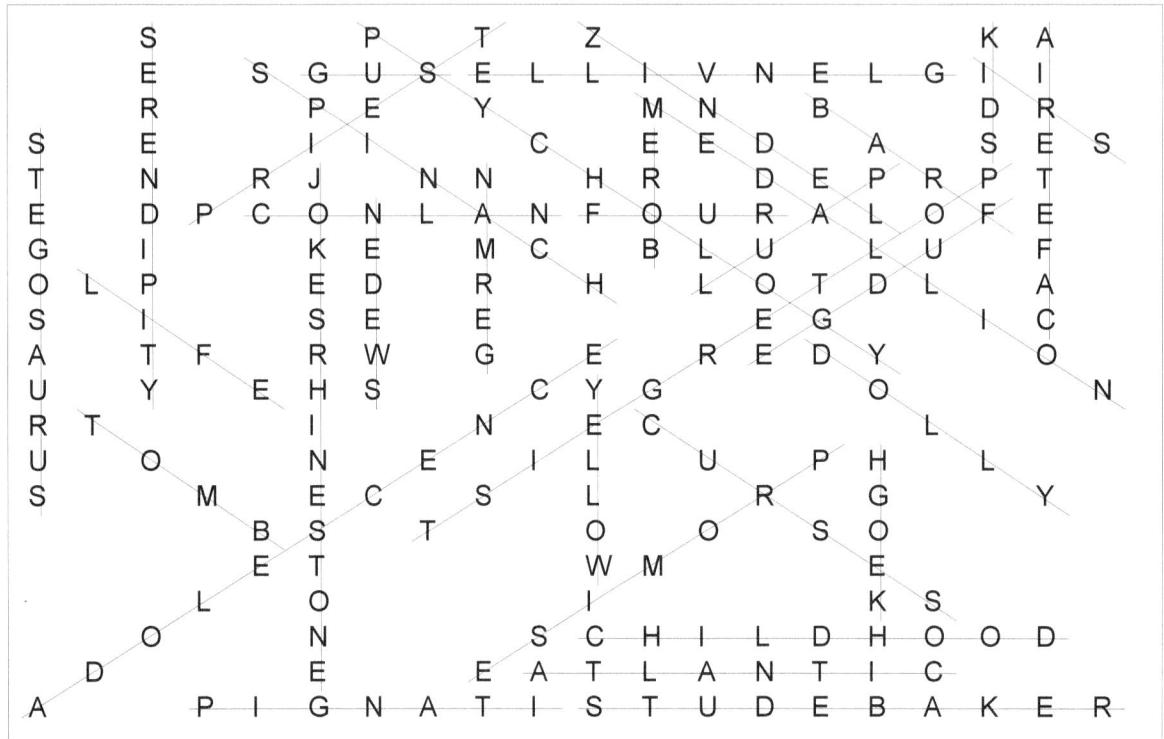

ADOLESCENCE	FOUR	LIFE	SERENDIPITY
ATLANTIC	FUDGE	MEDALLION	SPINACH
BARF	GERMAN	PAUL	STEGOSAURUS
BORE	GLENVILLE	PIGNATI	STUDEBAKER
CAFETERIA	GUS	POLTERGEIST	SWEDEN
CHILDHOOD	IRS	PRIEST	TOMB
CONLAN	JOKES	PROMISE	YELLOW
CURSES	KEOGH	PSYCHOLOGY	ZINDEL
DOLLY	KIDS	RHINESTONE	

Pigman's Legacy Crossword 1

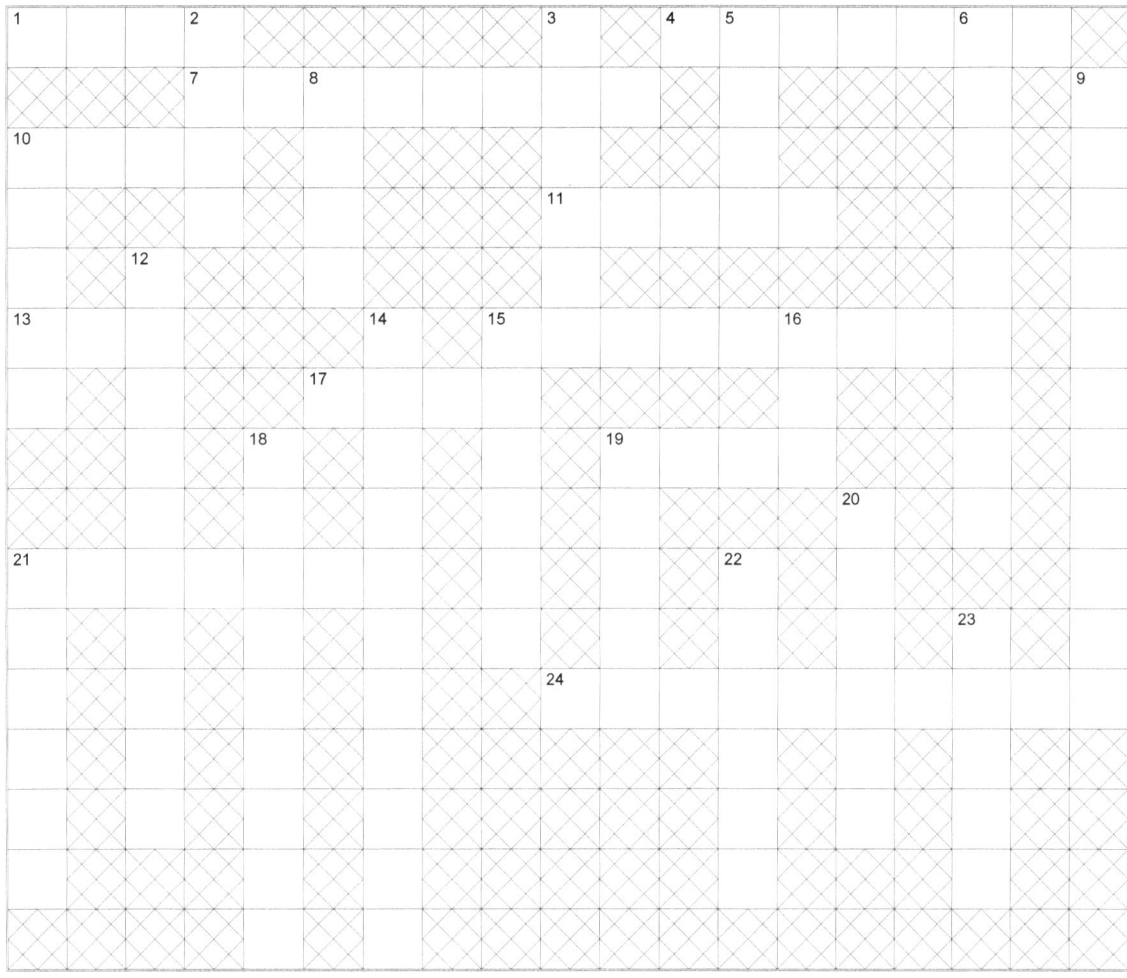

Across
1. A mausoleum is a large, stately ____.
4. Kind of cigarettes Lorraine wants John to smoke
7. The Colonel wanted to go to ____ City.
10. Dolly and the Colonel won ____ Thousand Dollars.
11. Ms. Racinski's first name
13. Phony name originally give by the Colonel
15. Colonel's real last name
17. How does John refer to his father?
19. How John and Lorraine refer to themselves
21. Name of the introduction to the book, The ____
24. Dolly wore what kind of earrings?

Down
2. Word John uses to be 'throw up'
3. Author's last name
5. First name of author
6. Dolly works in the school ____.
8. The only game the Colonel knows is The Game of ____.
9. Period from puberty to maturity
10. Gift that John and Lorraine took to the Colonel
12. Lorraine reads a lot of books about ____.
14. A mischievous ghost
15. Gus is a ____ Shepard.
16. What government agency does the Colonel fear most?
18. A Pigman basically kills a kid's ____.
19. A retirement plan for the self-employed.
20. What do @#$% and #@#$% represent in John's writing?
21. Who did the Colonel ask to see before he died?
22. John's last name
23. John no longer plays many practical ____.

Pigman's Legacy Crossword 1 Answer Key

	1 T	O	M	2 B				3 Z		4 S	5 P	I	N	A	6 C	H	
			7 A	T	8 L	A	N	T	I	C		A			A		9 A
10 F	O	U	R		I			N			U				F		D
U			F		F		11 D	O	L	L	Y				E		O
D		12 P			E		E								T		L
13 G	U	S			14 P	15 G	L	E	N	V	16 I	L	L	E		E
E		Y		17 B	O	R	E				R			R		S
		C	18 C	O	L	R		19 K	I	D	S			I		C
		H	H		T		M		E				20 C		A		E
21 P	R	O	M	I	S	E		A		O		22 C	U				N
R		L	L		R		N		G		O		R		23 J		C
I		O	D		G			24 R	H	I	N	E	S	T	O	N	E
E		G	H		E							L		E	K		
S		Y	O		I							A		S	E		
T			O		S							N			S		
			D		T												

Across
1. A mausoleum is a large, stately ____.
4. Kind of cigarettes Lorraine wants John to smoke
7. The Colonel wanted to go to ____ City.
10. Dolly and the Colonel won ____ Thousand Dollars.
11. Ms. Racinski's first name
13. Phony name originally give by the Colonel
15. Colonel's real last name
17. How does John refer to his father?
19. How John and Lorraine refer to themselves
21. Name of the introduction to the book, The ____
24. Dolly wore what kind of earrings?

Down
2. Word John uses to be 'throw up'
3. Author's last name
5. First name of author
6. Dolly works in the school ____.
8. The only game the Colonel knows is The Game of ____.
9. Period from puberty to maturity
10. Gift that John and Lorraine took to the Colonel
12. Lorraine reads a lot of books about ____.
14. A mischievous ghost
15. Gus is a ____ Shepard.
16. What government agency does the Colonel fear most?
18. A Pigman basically kills a kid's ____.
19. A retirement plan for the self-employed.
20. What do @#$% and #@#$% represent in John's writing?
21. Who did the Colonel ask to see before he died?
22. John's last name
23. John no longer plays many practical ____.

Pigman's Legacy Crossword 2

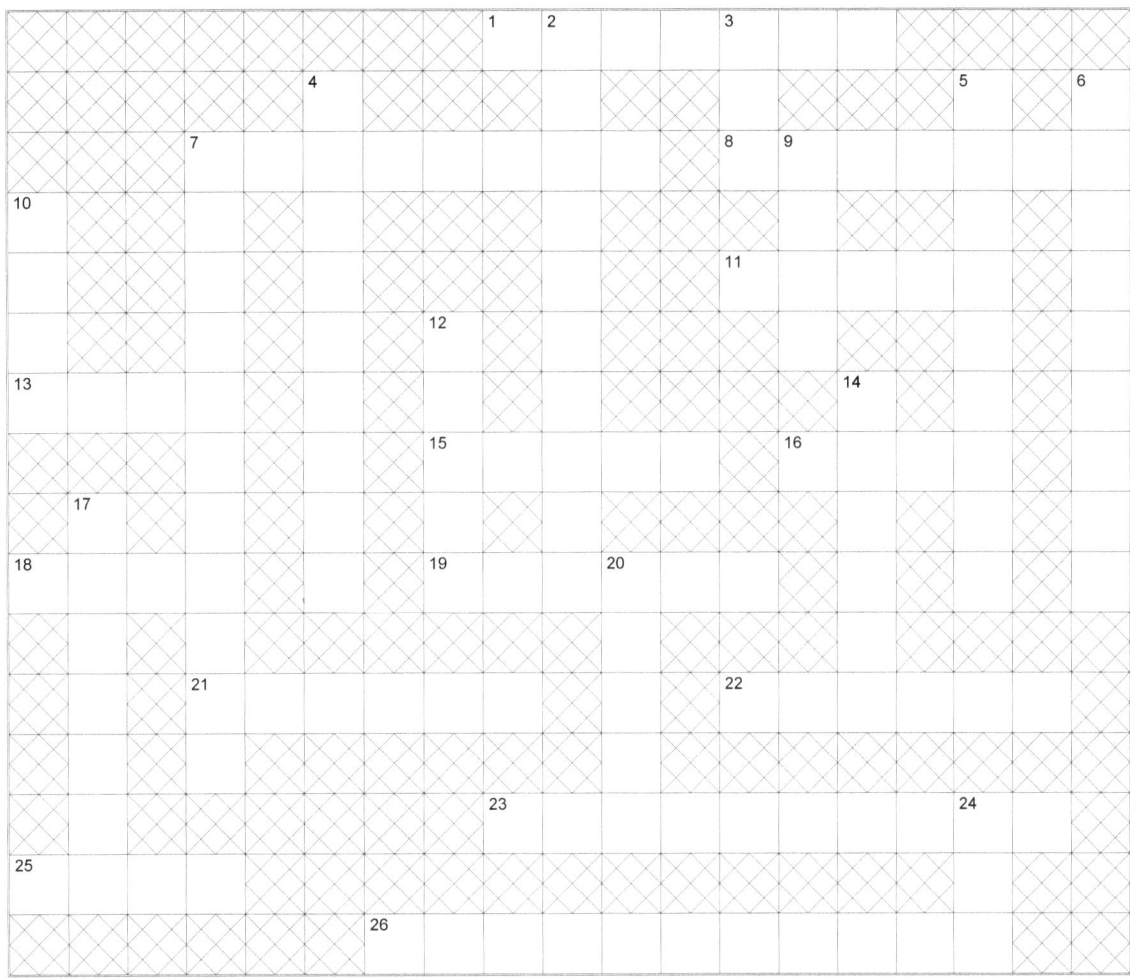

Across
1. Name of the introduction to the book, The ____
7. The Colonel wanted to go to ____ City.
8. Kind of cigarettes Lorraine wants John to smoke
11. Gift that John and Lorraine took to the Colonel
13. How does John refer to his father?
15. A retirement plan for the self-employed.
16. Dolly and the Colonel won ____ Thousand Dollars.
18. The only game the Colonel knows is The Game of ____.
19. The Colonel was knighted by the King of ____.
21. What do @#$% and #@#$% represent in John's writing?
22. Author's last name
23. Lorraine reads a lot of books about ____.
25. How John and Lorraine refer to themselves
26. Dinosaur with bony plates on its back

Down
2. Dolly wore what kind of earrings?
3. What government agency does the Colonel fear most?
4. Colonel's real last name
5. Dolly works in the school ____.
6. A Pigman basically kills a kid's ____.
7. Period from puberty to maturity
9. First name of author
10. A mausoleum is a large, stately ____.
12. John no longer plays many practical ____.
14. John's last name
17. Last name of the original Pigman
20. Ms. Racinski's first name
24. Phony name originally give by the Colonel

Pigman's Legacy Crossword 2 Answer Key

```
                    1 P  2 R  O   M   3 I  S   E
                4 G          H       R               5 C   6 C
             7 A  T   L   A  N  T   I   C   8 S  9 P  I  N  A  C  H
10 T            D         E           N           A         F         I
   O            D         N           E          11 F  U   D   G   E   L
   M            L         V  12 J     S           L            T        D
13 B  O   R   E           I     O     T                 14 C      E       H
                S         L  15 K  E  O   G   H     16 F   O   U   R   O
             17 P  C      L     E             N           N      I       O
18 L  I   F   E           E  19 S  W  20 D   E  N       L      A        D
      G           N                   O                   A
             21 N  C  U   R   S   E   S           22 Z    I   N   D   E   L
      A           E                   L
      T                       23 P  S  Y   C   H   O   L   24 G   Y
25 K  I   D   S                                                    U
                          26 S  T   E  G   O   S   A   U   R   U   S
```

Across
1. Name of the introduction to the book, The ____
7. The Colonel wanted to go to ____ City.
8. Kind of cigarettes Lorraine wants John to smoke
11. Gift that John and Lorraine took to the Colonel
13. How does John refer to his father?
15. A retirement plan for the self-employed.
16. Dolly and the Colonel won ____ Thousand Dollars.
18. The only game the Colonel knows is The Game of ____.
19. The Colonel was knighted by the King of ____.
21. What do @#$% and #@#$% represent in John's writing?
22. Author's last name
23. Lorraine reads a lot of books about ____.
25. How John and Lorraine refer to themselves
26. Dinosaur with bony plates on its back

Down
2. Dolly wore what kind of earrings?
3. What government agency does the Colonel fear most?
4. Colonel's real last name
5. Dolly works in the school ____.
6. A Pigman basically kills a kid's ____.
7. Period from puberty to maturity
9. First name of author
10. A mausoleum is a large, stately ____.
12. John no longer plays many practical ____.
14. John's last name
17. Last name of the original Pigman
20. Ms. Racinski's first name
24. Phony name originally give by the Colonel

Pigman's Legacy Crossword 3

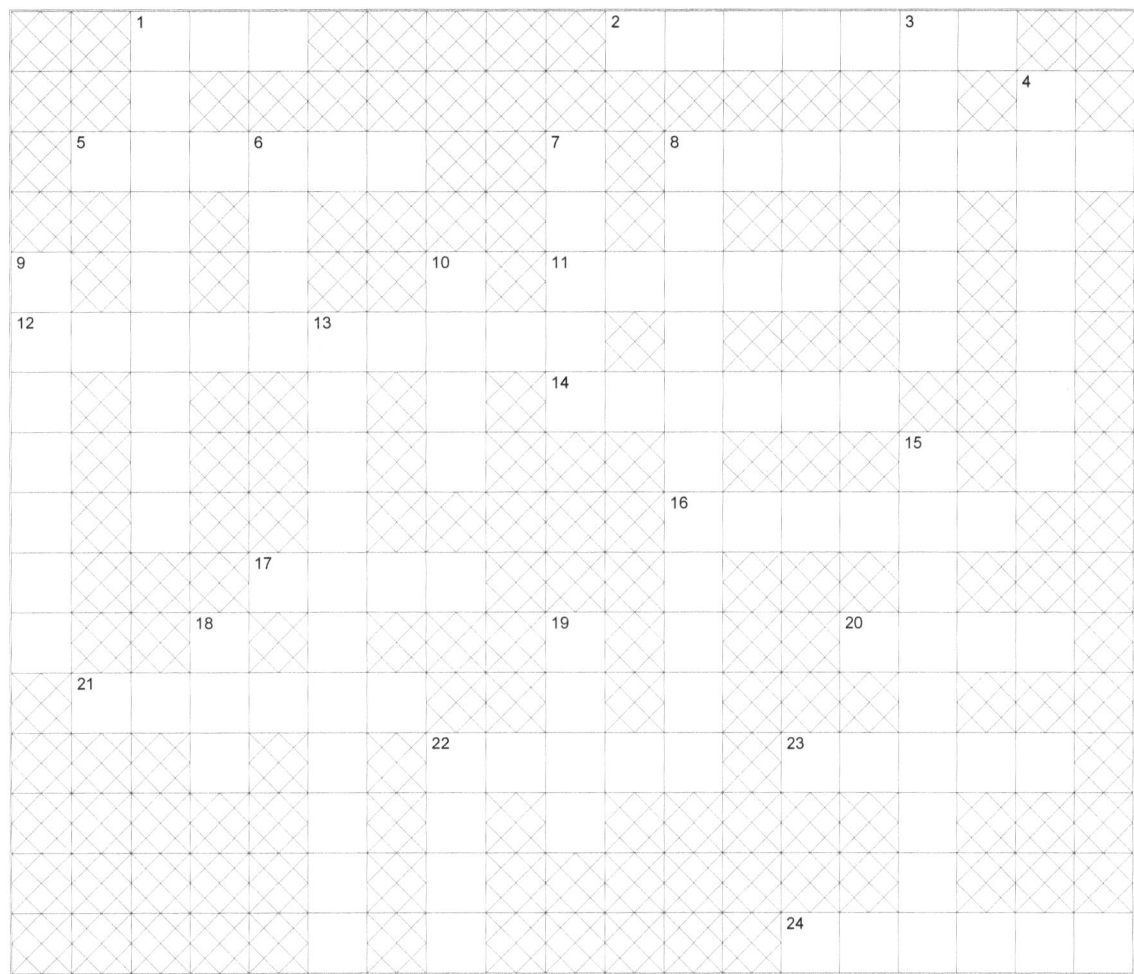

Across

1. Phony name originally give by the Colonel
2. Kind of cigarettes Lorraine wants John to smoke
5. Color of the Colonel's car
8. The Colonel wanted to go to ____ City.
11. A retirement plan for the self-employed.
12. Dolly wore what kind of earrings?
14. The Colonel was knighted by the King of ____.
16. What do @#$% and #@#$% represent in John's writing?
17. How does John refer to his father?
20. First name of author
21. Gus is a ____ Shepard.
22. Gift that John and Lorraine took to the Colonel
23. Ms. Racinski's first name
24. Author's last name

Down

1. Colonel's real last name
3. John's last name
4. Last name of the original Pigman
6. The only game the Colonel knows is The Game of ____.
7. John no longer plays many practical ____.
8. Period from puberty to maturity
9. Name of the introduction to the book, The ____
10. A mausoleum is a large, stately ____.
13. Dinosaur with bony plates on its back
15. What was the Colonel wearing around his neck?
18. What government agency does the Colonel fear most?
19. How John and Lorraine refer to themselves
22. Dolly and the Colonel won ____ Thousand Dollars.

Pigman's Legacy Crossword 3 Answer Key

		1 G	U	S				2 S	P	I	N	A	3 C	H	
		L											O		4 P
	5 Y	E	6 L	L	O	W		7 J	8 A	T	L	A	N	T	I	C
		N		I				O	D				L		G
9 P		V		F		10 T		11 K	E	O	G	H	A		N
12 R	H	I	N	E	S	T	O	N	E				N		A
O		L			T			14 S	W	E	D	E	N		T
M		L			E			S					15 M		I
I		E			G			16 C	U	R	S	E	S	
S			17 B	O	R	E		E					D	
E		18 I		S			19 K		N			20 P	A	U	L
	21 G	E	R	M	A	N		I		C			L	
		S		U		22 F	U	D	G	E		23 D	O	L	L	Y
				R		O		S				I	
				U		U						O	
				S		R					24 Z	I	N	D	E	L

Across

1. Phony name originally give by the Colonel
2. Kind of cigarettes Lorraine wants John to smoke
5. Color of the Colonel's car
8. The Colonel wanted to go to ____ City.
11. A retirement plan for the self-employed.
12. Dolly wore what kind of earrings?
14. The Colonel was knighted by the King of ____.
16. What do @#$% and #@#$% represent in John's writing?
17. How does John refer to his father?
20. First name of author
21. Gus is a ____ Shepard.
22. Gift that John and Lorraine took to the Colonel
23. Ms. Racinski's first name
24. Author's last name

Down

1. Colonel's real last name
3. John's last name
4. Last name of the original Pigman
6. The only game the Colonel knows is The Game of ____.
7. John no longer plays many practical ____.
8. Period from puberty to maturity
9. Name of the introduction to the book, The ____
10. A mausoleum is a large, stately ____.
13. Dinosaur with bony plates on its back
15. What was the Colonel wearing around his neck?
18. What government agency does the Colonel fear most?
19. How John and Lorraine refer to themselves
22. Dolly and the Colonel won ____ Thousand Dollars.

Pigman's Legacy Crossword 4

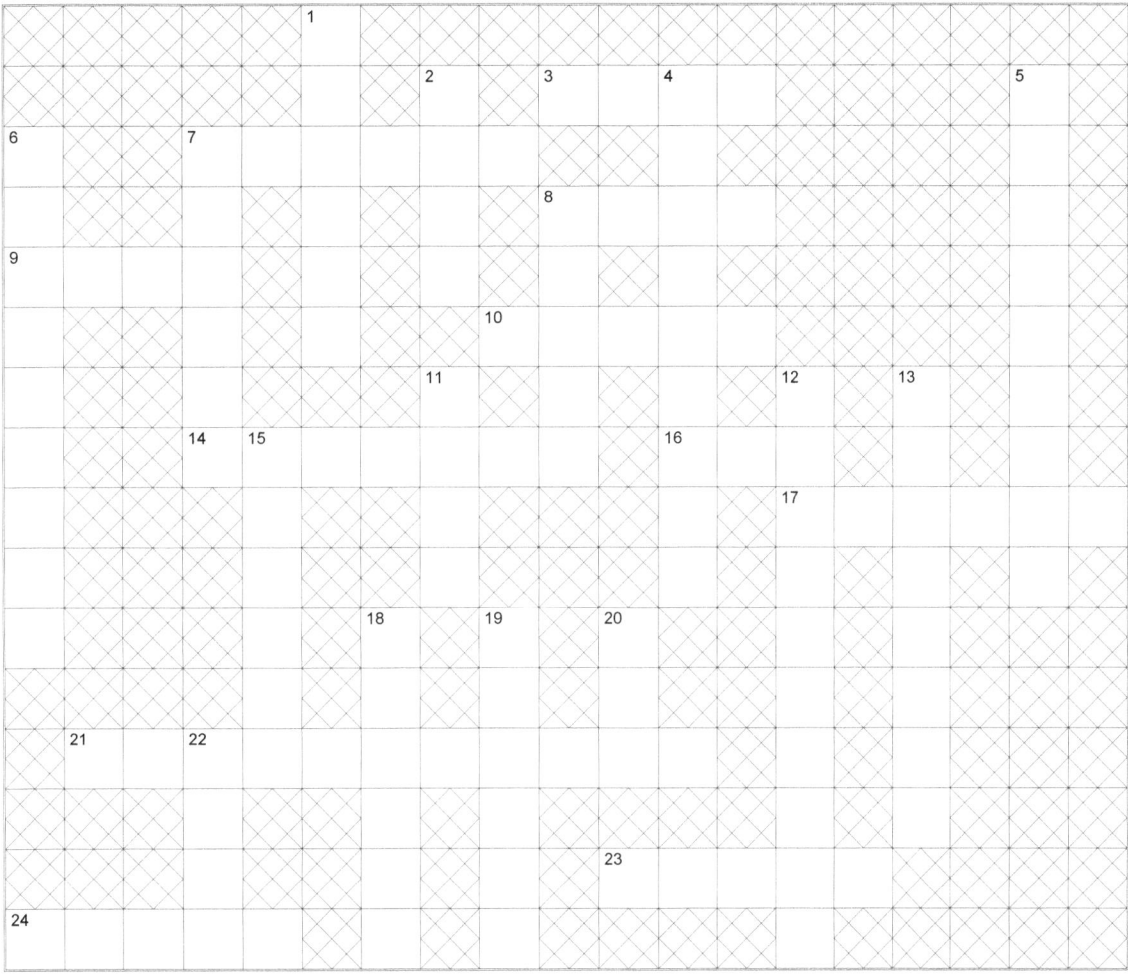

Across
3. A mausoleum is a large, stately ____.
7. John's last name
8. How John and Lorraine refer to themselves
9. Dolly and the Colonel won ____ Thousand Dollars.
10. Ms. Racinski's first name
14. Kind of cigarettes Lorraine wants John to smoke
16. What government agency does the Colonel fear most?
17. Color of the Colonel's car
21. A mischievous ghost
23. Gift that John and Lorraine took to the Colonel
24. John no longer plays many practical ____.

Down
1. Author's last name
2. First name of author
4. What was the Colonel wearing around his neck?
5. A Pigman basically kills a kid's ____.
6. Dolly works in the school ____.
7. What do @#$% and #@#$% represent in John's writing?
8. A retirement plan for the self-employed.
11. Word John uses to be 'throw up'
12. Lorraine reads a lot of books about ____.
13. The Colonel wanted to go to ____ City.
15. Who did the Colonel ask to see before he died?
18. Gus is a ____ Shepard.
19. The Colonel was knighted by the King of ____.
20. Phony name originally give by the Colonel
22. The only game the Colonel knows is The Game of ____.

Pigman's Legacy Crossword 4 Answer Key

					1 Z							
				I	2 P	3 T	O	4 M	B		5 C	
6 C		7 C	O	N	L	A	N		E		H	
A		U		D		U	8 K	I	D	S	I	
9 F	O	U	R		E		L	E	A		L	
E		O	S		L		10 D	O	L	L	Y	D
T		E			11 B		G		L	12 P	13 A	H
E	14 S	15 P	I	N	A	C	H		16 I	R	S	T	O
R		R			R				O		17 Y	E	L	L	O	W
I		I			F				N		C		A		D	
A		E		18 G		19 S		20 G		H		N				
		S		E		W		U		O		T				
	21 P	22 O	L	T	E	R	G	E	I	S	T	L		I		
		I		M		D						O		C		
		F		A		E		23 F	U	D	G	E				
24 J	O	K	E	S		N		N				Y				

Across
3. A mausoleum is a large, stately ____.
7. John's last name
8. How John and Lorraine refer to themselves
9. Dolly and the Colonel won ____ Thousand Dollars.
10. Ms. Racinski's first name
14. Kind of cigarettes Lorraine wants John to smoke
16. What government agency does the Colonel fear most?
17. Color of the Colonel's car
21. A mischievous ghost
23. Gift that John and Lorraine took to the Colonel
24. John no longer plays many practical ____.

Down
1. Author's last name
2. First name of author
4. What was the Colonel wearing around his neck?
5. A Pigman basically kills a kid's ____.
6. Dolly works in the school ____.
7. What do @#$% and #@#$% represent in John's writing?
8. A retirement plan for the self-employed.
11. Word John uses to be 'throw up'
12. Lorraine reads a lot of books about ____.
13. The Colonel wanted to go to ____ City.
15. Who did the Colonel ask to see before he died?
18. Gus is a ____ Shepard.
19. The Colonel was knighted by the King of ____.
20. Phony name originally give by the Colonel
22. The only game the Colonel knows is The Game of ____.

Pigman's Legacy

GUS	STEGOSAURUS	RHINESTONE	PRIEST	IRS
POLTERGEIST	ADOLESCENCE	PSYCHOLOGY	PROMISE	PAUL
CURSES	DOLLY	FREE SPACE	MEDALLION	KIDS
GERMAN	SWEDEN	ZINDEL	CAFETERIA	BORE
SPINACH	TOMB	BARF	ATLANTIC	CHILDHOOD

Pigman's Legacy

KEOGH	FUDGE	STUDEBAKER	PIGNATI	YELLOW
GLENVILLE	LIFE	JOKES	CONLAN	FOUR
CHILDHOOD	ATLANTIC	FREE SPACE	TOMB	SPINACH
BORE	CAFETERIA	ZINDEL	SWEDEN	GERMAN
KIDS	MEDALLION	SERENDIPITY	DOLLY	CURSES

Pigman's Legacy

CHILDHOOD	FUDGE	GERMAN	KIDS	PIGNATI
IRS	RHINESTONE	PAUL	GLENVILLE	TOMB
STUDEBAKER	ADOLESCENCE	FREE SPACE	SPINACH	LIFE
YELLOW	SWEDEN	STEGOSAURUS	JOKES	ZINDEL
KEOGH	GUS	PSYCHOLOGY	BARF	POLTERGEIST

Pigman's Legacy

CURSES	CONLAN	FOUR	CAFETERIA	BORE
MEDALLION	SERENDIPITY	ATLANTIC	PRIEST	PROMISE
POLTERGEIST	BARF	FREE SPACE	GUS	KEOGH
ZINDEL	JOKES	STEGOSAURUS	SWEDEN	YELLOW
LIFE	SPINACH	DOLLY	ADOLESCENCE	STUDEBAKER

Pigman's Legacy

SERENDIPITY	DOLLY	GUS	PIGNATI	CAFETERIA
IRS	STUDEBAKER	PAUL	PRIEST	BARF
LIFE	BORE	FREE SPACE	CURSES	FUDGE
KEOGH	ADOLESCENCE	STEGOSAURUS	SWEDEN	JOKES
GLENVILLE	RHINESTONE	CONLAN	YELLOW	TOMB

Pigman's Legacy

PROMISE	MEDALLION	KIDS	CHILDHOOD	POLTERGEIST
ATLANTIC	FOUR	ZINDEL	GERMAN	SPINACH
TOMB	YELLOW	FREE SPACE	RHINESTONE	GLENVILLE
JOKES	SWEDEN	STEGOSAURUS	ADOLESCENCE	KEOGH
FUDGE	CURSES	PSYCHOLOGY	BORE	LIFE

Pigman's Legacy

RHINESTONE	PAUL	MEDALLION	CURSES	CAFETERIA
CONLAN	STUDEBAKER	SERENDIPITY	KEOGH	DOLLY
PROMISE	STEGOSAURUS	FREE SPACE	PIGNATI	ZINDEL
BARF	YELLOW	CHILDHOOD	PSYCHOLOGY	SWEDEN
IRS	PRIEST	ADOLESCENCE	BORE	GLENVILLE

Pigman's Legacy

KIDS	FUDGE	FOUR	GERMAN	POLTERGEIST
ATLANTIC	GUS	LIFE	JOKES	TOMB
GLENVILLE	BORE	FREE SPACE	PRIEST	IRS
SWEDEN	PSYCHOLOGY	CHILDHOOD	YELLOW	BARF
ZINDEL	PIGNATI	SPINACH	STEGOSAURUS	PROMISE

Pigman's Legacy

DOLLY	CONLAN	GLENVILLE	POLTERGEIST	BARF
CHILDHOOD	TOMB	ATLANTIC	JOKES	GERMAN
IRS	SPINACH	FREE SPACE	PIGNATI	CAFETERIA
LIFE	BORE	YELLOW	KIDS	FOUR
ZINDEL	FUDGE	GUS	STEGOSAURUS	PRIEST

Pigman's Legacy

PSYCHOLOGY	RHINESTONE	CURSES	ADOLESCENCE	SERENDIPITY
PAUL	SWEDEN	KEOGH	PROMISE	MEDALLION
PRIEST	STEGOSAURUS	FREE SPACE	FUDGE	ZINDEL
FOUR	KIDS	YELLOW	BORE	LIFE
CAFETERIA	PIGNATI	STUDEBAKER	SPINACH	IRS

Pigman's Legacy

BARF	POLTERGEIST	PRIEST	GUS	JOKES
ATLANTIC	ZINDEL	STEGOSAURUS	CHILDHOOD	PAUL
SWEDEN	TOMB	FREE SPACE	GLENVILLE	SERENDIPITY
FUDGE	ADOLESCENCE	FOUR	YELLOW	KEOGH
PROMISE	CURSES	LIFE	KIDS	PSYCHOLOGY

Pigman's Legacy

RHINESTONE	PIGNATI	CAFETERIA	GERMAN	MEDALLION
IRS	CONLAN	DOLLY	STUDEBAKER	BORE
PSYCHOLOGY	KIDS	FREE SPACE	CURSES	PROMISE
KEOGH	YELLOW	FOUR	ADOLESCENCE	FUDGE
SERENDIPITY	GLENVILLE	SPINACH	TOMB	SWEDEN

Pigman's Legacy

TOMB	CHILDHOOD	PRIEST	FOUR	MEDALLION
PSYCHOLOGY	KIDS	ADOLESCENCE	GLENVILLE	PIGNATI
DOLLY	STUDEBAKER	FREE SPACE	POLTERGEIST	GERMAN
SPINACH	FUDGE	PAUL	BARF	PROMISE
SWEDEN	BORE	SERENDIPITY	GUS	RHINESTONE

Pigman's Legacy

CURSES	ZINDEL	CAFETERIA	KEOGH	JOKES
ATLANTIC	IRS	LIFE	YELLOW	STEGOSAURUS
RHINESTONE	GUS	FREE SPACE	BORE	SWEDEN
PROMISE	BARF	PAUL	FUDGE	SPINACH
GERMAN	POLTERGEIST	CONLAN	STUDEBAKER	DOLLY

Pigman's Legacy

PIGNATI	PROMISE	GUS	SERENDIPITY	FUDGE
POLTERGEIST	ATLANTIC	KIDS	CHILDHOOD	YELLOW
MEDALLION	ADOLESCENCE	FREE SPACE	BARF	PAUL
ZINDEL	DOLLY	CURSES	RHINESTONE	GERMAN
PSYCHOLOGY	STUDEBAKER	LIFE	CAFETERIA	JOKES

Pigman's Legacy

CONLAN	PRIEST	BORE	IRS	SWEDEN
FOUR	STEGOSAURUS	TOMB	KEOGH	GLENVILLE
JOKES	CAFETERIA	FREE SPACE	STUDEBAKER	PSYCHOLOGY
GERMAN	RHINESTONE	CURSES	DOLLY	ZINDEL
PAUL	BARF	SPINACH	ADOLESCENCE	MEDALLION

Pigman's Legacy

DOLLY	CAFETERIA	PIGNATI	JOKES	POLTERGEIST
TOMB	GERMAN	SWEDEN	ZINDEL	BARF
RHINESTONE	LIFE	FREE SPACE	PAUL	KEOGH
IRS	CONLAN	FOUR	CHILDHOOD	ATLANTIC
KIDS	CURSES	PROMISE	STEGOSAURUS	SPINACH

Pigman's Legacy

PSYCHOLOGY	GLENVILLE	BORE	FUDGE	ADOLESCENCE
PRIEST	MEDALLION	SERENDIPITY	GUS	YELLOW
SPINACH	STEGOSAURUS	FREE SPACE	CURSES	KIDS
ATLANTIC	CHILDHOOD	FOUR	CONLAN	IRS
KEOGH	PAUL	STUDEBAKER	LIFE	RHINESTONE

Pigman's Legacy

CHILDHOOD	FOUR	DOLLY	ATLANTIC	CONLAN
CAFETERIA	BARF	GERMAN	RHINESTONE	STUDEBAKER
LIFE	GUS	FREE SPACE	ZINDEL	MEDALLION
GLENVILLE	PRIEST	POLTERGEIST	ADOLESCENCE	SERENDIPITY
CURSES	PSYCHOLOGY	YELLOW	TOMB	FUDGE

Pigman's Legacy

STEGOSAURUS	PIGNATI	SPINACH	BORE	JOKES
PAUL	SWEDEN	KEOGH	KIDS	IRS
FUDGE	TOMB	FREE SPACE	PSYCHOLOGY	CURSES
SERENDIPITY	ADOLESCENCE	POLTERGEIST	PRIEST	GLENVILLE
MEDALLION	ZINDEL	PROMISE	GUS	LIFE

Pigman's Legacy

KEOGH	FUDGE	BORE	ADOLESCENCE	PSYCHOLOGY
STEGOSAURUS	ZINDEL	DOLLY	KIDS	PRIEST
CURSES	POLTERGEIST	FREE SPACE	JOKES	GLENVILLE
FOUR	BARF	IRS	GERMAN	CAFETERIA
SPINACH	MEDALLION	CHILDHOOD	STUDEBAKER	PAUL

Pigman's Legacy

CONLAN	TOMB	PROMISE	LIFE	YELLOW
GUS	PIGNATI	ATLANTIC	RHINESTONE	SERENDIPITY
PAUL	STUDEBAKER	FREE SPACE	MEDALLION	SPINACH
CAFETERIA	GERMAN	IRS	BARF	FOUR
GLENVILLE	JOKES	SWEDEN	POLTERGEIST	CURSES

Pigman's Legacy

ADOLESCENCE	PRIEST	STEGOSAURUS	CONLAN	SWEDEN
CAFETERIA	KEOGH	FUDGE	CHILDHOOD	PIGNATI
IRS	CURSES	FREE SPACE	ATLANTIC	ZINDEL
GUS	GLENVILLE	GERMAN	PAUL	TOMB
LIFE	POLTERGEIST	DOLLY	SERENDIPITY	BORE

Pigman's Legacy

PSYCHOLOGY	SPINACH	FOUR	PROMISE	YELLOW
STUDEBAKER	BARF	MEDALLION	KIDS	JOKES
BORE	SERENDIPITY	FREE SPACE	POLTERGEIST	LIFE
TOMB	PAUL	GERMAN	GLENVILLE	GUS
ZINDEL	ATLANTIC	RHINESTONE	CURSES	IRS

Pigman's Legacy

SERENDIPITY	GUS	SPINACH	PIGNATI	MEDALLION
KEOGH	DOLLY	PRIEST	FUDGE	LIFE
SWEDEN	CURSES	FREE SPACE	CAFETERIA	GERMAN
YELLOW	ADOLESCENCE	ZINDEL	ATLANTIC	FOUR
PROMISE	POLTERGEIST	IRS	CONLAN	CHILDHOOD

Pigman's Legacy

BARF	STUDEBAKER	GLENVILLE	RHINESTONE	PAUL
PSYCHOLOGY	STEGOSAURUS	TOMB	BORE	KIDS
CHILDHOOD	CONLAN	FREE SPACE	POLTERGEIST	PROMISE
FOUR	ATLANTIC	ZINDEL	ADOLESCENCE	YELLOW
GERMAN	CAFETERIA	JOKES	CURSES	SWEDEN

Pigman's Legacy

TOMB	IRS	SWEDEN	YELLOW	STUDEBAKER
PSYCHOLOGY	FOUR	PROMISE	STEGOSAURUS	BARF
MEDALLION	GUS	FREE SPACE	PAUL	KEOGH
ADOLESCENCE	CONLAN	GERMAN	KIDS	LIFE
ATLANTIC	CHILDHOOD	ZINDEL	CURSES	POLTERGEIST

Pigman's Legacy

FUDGE	DOLLY	SPINACH	SERENDIPITY	BORE
PRIEST	PIGNATI	GLENVILLE	RHINESTONE	CAFETERIA
POLTERGEIST	CURSES	FREE SPACE	CHILDHOOD	ATLANTIC
LIFE	KIDS	GERMAN	CONLAN	ADOLESCENCE
KEOGH	PAUL	JOKES	GUS	MEDALLION

Pigman's Legacy

CAFETERIA	GERMAN	GUS	MEDALLION	CHILDHOOD
TOMB	PAUL	PIGNATI	PROMISE	RHINESTONE
CONLAN	BORE	FREE SPACE	SWEDEN	CURSES
JOKES	IRS	SERENDIPITY	KIDS	BARF
STEGOSAURUS	DOLLY	GLENVILLE	SPINACH	PRIEST

Pigman's Legacy

ZINDEL	POLTERGEIST	FUDGE	ATLANTIC	KEOGH
FOUR	STUDEBAKER	PSYCHOLOGY	LIFE	YELLOW
PRIEST	SPINACH	FREE SPACE	DOLLY	STEGOSAURUS
BARF	KIDS	SERENDIPITY	IRS	JOKES
CURSES	SWEDEN	ADOLESCENCE	BORE	CONLAN

Pigman's Legacy

ADOLESCENCE	BARF	KEOGH	TOMB	STEGOSAURUS
BORE	JOKES	MEDALLION	LIFE	SPINACH
CONLAN	PSYCHOLOGY	FREE SPACE	GUS	GLENVILLE
PAUL	POLTERGEIST	ATLANTIC	CHILDHOOD	PRIEST
FOUR	PROMISE	SERENDIPITY	GERMAN	PIGNATI

Pigman's Legacy

KIDS	STUDEBAKER	SWEDEN	ZINDEL	RHINESTONE
IRS	YELLOW	FUDGE	CURSES	CAFETERIA
PIGNATI	GERMAN	FREE SPACE	PROMISE	FOUR
PRIEST	CHILDHOOD	ATLANTIC	POLTERGEIST	PAUL
GLENVILLE	GUS	DOLLY	PSYCHOLOGY	CONLAN

Pigman's Legacy Vocabulary Word List

No.	Word	Clue/Definition
1.	ABSTINENCE	Deliberate restraining of oneself; not indulging
2.	ADOLESCENCE	Period from puberty to maturity; teen years
3.	ANGUISH	Agonizing physical or mental pain
4.	APPARITION	A ghost
5.	BLURTED	Said
6.	CONDONE	Overlook; forgive; disregard
7.	CONVENT	A monastic community or house, especially of nuns
8.	CONVICTION	Strong belief
9.	DILAPIDATED	In disrepair, deterioration, or ruin
10.	DISCIPLE	Assistant; follower
11.	DOSSIER	Collection of papers about a particular person
12.	ECSTASY	Delight
13.	ENGRAVED	Carved or etched into a surface
14.	EPIC	Literary work that suggests grandeur or heroics
15.	FLEECING	Defrauding of money or property; swindling
16.	FOIBLES	Minor weaknesses or failings of character
17.	FOSSIL	Skeleton or leaf imprint
18.	FRAIL	Not substantial; slight
19.	GEOLOGY	Science of the origin, history and structure of the earth
20.	GRAFFITI	Drawing or inscription on wall or other surface
21.	GRUFF	Brief and unfriendly; harsh
22.	IGNITED	Lit up
23.	IMMERSE	Cover completely in something else
24.	INDIGENT	Impoverished; needy
25.	INSTINCTIVE	Impulsive
26.	INVERTED	Turned inside out or up and down
27.	KEOGH	Retirement plan for the self-employed
28.	LEGACY	Something handed down, as from an ancestor
29.	LIMITATIONS	Restrictions; boundaries
30.	MANNEQUINS	Dummies
31.	MAUSOLEUM	A large stately tomb
32.	MEDALLION	A large medal
33.	MEDICARE	Government program for medical care for those over 65
34.	MEMORIAL	Commemorating, serving as a reminder of
35.	MESMERIZED	Hypnotized
36.	MORTIFIED	Humiliated; shamed
37.	MUTE	Silent; unable to speak
38.	NAIVE	Simple; lacking in worldliness and sophistication
39.	OMEN	Sigh of future good or evil
40.	PERKILY	In a lively way
41.	PETRIFY	Come to become stonelike; to deaden
42.	PLATONICALLY	Transcending physical desire; spiritual
43.	PSYCHOLOGY	Science that deals with mental processes and behavior
44.	PUBESCENT	Reaching or having reached puberty
45.	REFINERIES	Plants that purify crude substances
46.	REGRETS	Feels sorry about
47.	REINCARNATED	Reborn
48.	REVERIE	A state of abstract musing
49.	RHINESTONE	A colorless artificial gem of paste or glass
50.	SERENDIPITY	Ability to make fortunate discoveries by accident
51.	SHRINE	Site revered for its associations

Pigman's Legacy Vocabulary Word List Continued

No. Word	Clue/Definition
52. SQUATTING	Settling without legal claim
53. STEGOSAURUS	Dinosaur with a double row of bony plates on its back
54. STIMULATING	Exciting
55. STUPOR	Daze
56. SUBMERGED	Under; beneath
57. SURREPTITIOUSLY	Secretly
58. THROMBOSIS	Formation of blood clot in a vessel or the heart
59. TRESPASSING	Invading the property rights of another
60. UNDULATING	Making a wavelike movement
61. VISION	Experience of seeing the supernatural as if with the eyes
62. VIVACIOUSNESS	Liveliness; spiritedness; animation
63. WHEEZE	Hoarse whistling sound
64. WIDOW	Woman whose husband has died
65. ZOMBIES	People who look and behave like robots

Pigman's Legacy Vocabulary Fill In The Blanks 1

1. Literary work that suggests grandeur or heroics
2. Impulsive
3. Period from puberty to maturity; teen years
4. Impoverished; needy
5. Collection of papers about a particular person
6. Agonizing physical or mental pain
7. Hoarse whistling sound
8. Come to become stonelike; to deaden
9. Settling without legal claim
10. Hypnotized
11. Science of the origin, history and structure of the earth
12. Reborn
13. Reaching or having reached puberty
14. Brief and unfriendly; harsh
15. A large stately tomb
16. Deliberate restraining of oneself; not indulging
17. Simple; lacking in worldliness and sophistication
18. Making a wavelike movement
19. Experience of seeing the supernatural as if with the eyes
20. Restrictions; boundaries

Pigman's Legacy Vocabulary Fill In The Blanks 1 Answer Key

EPIC	1. Literary work that suggests grandeur or heroics
INSTINCTIVE	2. Impulsive
ADOLESCENCE	3. Period from puberty to maturity; teen years
INDIGENT	4. Impoverished; needy
DOSSIER	5. Collection of papers about a particular person
ANGUISH	6. Agonizing physical or mental pain
WHEEZE	7. Hoarse whistling sound
PETRIFY	8. Come to become stonelike; to deaden
SQUATTING	9. Settling without legal claim
MESMERIZED	10. Hypnotized
GEOLOGY	11. Science of the origin, history and structure of the earth
REINCARNATED	12. Reborn
PUBESCENT	13. Reaching or having reached puberty
GRUFF	14. Brief and unfriendly; harsh
MAUSOLEUM	15. A large stately tomb
ABSTINENCE	16. Deliberate restraining of oneself; not indulging
NAIVE	17. Simple; lacking in worldliness and sophistication
UNDULATING	18. Making a wavelike movement
VISION	19. Experience of seeing the supernatural as if with the eyes
LIMITATIONS	20. Restrictions; boundaries

Pigman's Legacy Vocabulary Fill In The Blanks 2

1. Science that deals with mental processes and behavior
2. Skeleton or leaf imprint
3. Under; beneath
4. Ability to make fortunate discoveries by accident
5. Overlook; forgive; disregard
6. Retirement plan for the self-employed
7. Sigh of future good or evil
8. Brief and unfriendly; harsh
9. Settling without legal claim
10. Collection of papers about a particular person
11. A state of abstract musing
12. Dinosaur with a double row of bony plates on its back
13. A ghost
14. People who look and behave like robots
15. Invading the property rights of another
16. Restrictions; boundaries
17. Daze
18. A large medal
19. A monastic community or house, especially of nuns
20. Simple; lacking in worldliness and sophistication

Pigman's Legacy Vocabulary Fill In The Blanks 2 Answer Key

PSYCHOLOGY	1. Science that deals with mental processes and behavior
FOSSIL	2. Skeleton or leaf imprint
SUBMERGED	3. Under; beneath
SERENDIPITY	4. Ability to make fortunate discoveries by accident
CONDONE	5. Overlook; forgive; disregard
KEOGH	6. Retirement plan for the self-employed
OMEN	7. Sigh of future good or evil
GRUFF	8. Brief and unfriendly; harsh
SQUATTING	9. Settling without legal claim
DOSSIER	10. Collection of papers about a particular person
REVERIE	11. A state of abstract musing
STEGOSAURUS	12. Dinosaur with a double row of bony plates on its back
APPARITION	13. A ghost
ZOMBIES	14. People who look and behave like robots
TRESPASSING	15. Invading the property rights of another
LIMITATIONS	16. Restrictions; boundaries
STUPOR	17. Daze
MEDALLION	18. A large medal
CONVENT	19. A monastic community or house, especially of nuns
NAIVE	20. Simple; lacking in worldliness and sophistication

Pigman's Legacy Vocabulary Fill In The Blanks 3

1. Come to become stonelike; to deaden
2. Daze
3. A monastic community or house, especially of nuns
4. Commemorating, serving as a reminder of
5. Ability to make fortunate discoveries by accident
6. Turned inside out or up and down
7. Impoverished; needy
8. Science of the origin, history and structure of the earth
9. Not substantial; slight
10. Simple; lacking in worldliness and sophistication
11. Transcending physical desire; spiritual
12. Liveliness; spiritedness; animation
13. A state of abstract musing
14. In a lively way
15. Plants that purify crude substances
16. Science that deals with mental processes and behavior
17. A large stately tomb
18. Woman whose husband has died
19. Impulsive
20. Secretly

Pigman's Legacy Vocabulary Fill In The Blanks 3 Answer Key

PETRIFY	1. Come to become stonelike; to deaden
STUPOR	2. Daze
CONVENT	3. A monastic community or house, especially of nuns
MEMORIAL	4. Commemorating, serving as a reminder of
SERENDIPITY	5. Ability to make fortunate discoveries by accident
INVERTED	6. Turned inside out or up and down
INDIGENT	7. Impoverished; needy
GEOLOGY	8. Science of the origin, history and structure of the earth
FRAIL	9. Not substantial; slight
NAIVE	10. Simple; lacking in worldliness and sophistication
PLATONICALLY	11. Transcending physical desire; spiritual
VIVACIOUSNESS	12. Liveliness; spiritedness; animation
REVERIE	13. A state of abstract musing
PERKILY	14. In a lively way
REFINERIES	15. Plants that purify crude substances
PSYCHOLOGY	16. Science that deals with mental processes and behavior
MAUSOLEUM	17. A large stately tomb
WIDOW	18. Woman whose husband has died
INSTINCTIVE	19. Impulsive
SURREPTITIOUSLY	20. Secretly

Pigman's Legacy Vocabulary Fill In The Blanks 4

1. People who look and behave like robots
2. Hoarse whistling sound
3. Overlook; forgive; disregard
4. Commemorating, serving as a reminder of
5. Making a wavelike movement
6. Impulsive
7. Exciting
8. Dinosaur with a double row of bony plates on its back
9. A ghost
10. Reborn
11. Collection of papers about a particular person
12. Humiliated; shamed
13. Deliberate restraining of oneself; not indulging
14. Liveliness; spiritedness; animation
15. Period from puberty to maturity; teen years
16. Science of the origin, history and structure of the earth
17. Daze
18. Experience of seeing the supernatural as if with the eyes
19. Reaching or having reached puberty
20. Lit up

Pigman's Legacy Vocabulary Fill In The Blanks 4 Answer Key

ZOMBIES	1. People who look and behave like robots
WHEEZE	2. Hoarse whistling sound
CONDONE	3. Overlook; forgive; disregard
MEMORIAL	4. Commemorating, serving as a reminder of
UNDULATING	5. Making a wavelike movement
INSTINCTIVE	6. Impulsive
STIMULATING	7. Exciting
STEGOSAURUS	8. Dinosaur with a double row of bony plates on its back
APPARITION	9. A ghost
REINCARNATED	10. Reborn
DOSSIER	11. Collection of papers about a particular person
MORTIFIED	12. Humiliated; shamed
ABSTINENCE	13. Deliberate restraining of oneself; not indulging
VIVACIOUSNESS	14. Liveliness; spiritedness; animation
ADOLESCENCE	15. Period from puberty to maturity; teen years
GEOLOGY	16. Science of the origin, history and structure of the earth
STUPOR	17. Daze
VISION	18. Experience of seeing the supernatural as if with the eyes
PUBESCENT	19. Reaching or having reached puberty
IGNITED	20. Lit up

Pigman's Legacy Vocabulary Matching 1

___ 1. DOSSIER
___ 2. CONVICTION
___ 3. MUTE
___ 4. MANNEQUINS
___ 5. UNDULATING
___ 6. MEDALLION
___ 7. MESMERIZED
___ 8. STIMULATING
___ 9. REVERIE
___ 10. GRUFF
___ 11. FOIBLES
___ 12. MEMORIAL
___ 13. ANGUISH
___ 14. SURREPTITIOUSLY
___ 15. FLEECING
___ 16. PUBESCENT
___ 17. TRESPASSING
___ 18. REGRETS
___ 19. SHRINE
___ 20. PETRIFY
___ 21. MEDICARE
___ 22. STUPOR
___ 23. PSYCHOLOGY
___ 24. NAIVE
___ 25. BLURTED

A. Collection of papers about a particular person
B. Dummies
C. Secretly
D. Come to become stonelike; to deaden
E. Invading the property rights of another
F. Government program for medical care for those over 65
G. Commemorating, serving as a reminder of
H. Simple; lacking in worldliness and sophistication
I. Brief and unfriendly; harsh
J. A large medal
K. Site revered for its associations
L. Agonizing physical or mental pain
M. Minor weaknesses or failings of character
N. Said
O. Making a wavelike movement
P. Daze
Q. Reaching or having reached puberty
R. Science that deals with mental processes and behavior
S. Exciting
T. Silent; unable to speak
U. Defrauding of money or property; swindling
V. Feels sorry about
W. A state of abstract musing
X. Hypnotized
Y. Strong belief

Pigman's Legacy Vocabulary Matching 1 Answer Key

A - 1. DOSSIER	A. Collection of papers about a particular person
Y - 2. CONVICTION	B. Dummies
T - 3. MUTE	C. Secretly
B - 4. MANNEQUINS	D. Come to become stonelike; to deaden
O - 5. UNDULATING	E. Invading the property rights of another
J - 6. MEDALLION	F. Government program for medical care for those over 65
X - 7. MESMERIZED	G. Commemorating, serving as a reminder of
S - 8. STIMULATING	H. Simple; lacking in worldliness and sophistication
W - 9. REVERIE	I. Brief and unfriendly; harsh
I - 10. GRUFF	J. A large medal
M - 11. FOIBLES	K. Site revered for its associations
G - 12. MEMORIAL	L. Agonizing physical or mental pain
L - 13. ANGUISH	M. Minor weaknesses or failings of character
C - 14. SURREPTITIOUSLY	N. Said
U - 15. FLEECING	O. Making a wavelike movement
Q - 16. PUBESCENT	P. Daze
E - 17. TRESPASSING	Q. Reaching or having reached puberty
V - 18. REGRETS	R. Science that deals with mental processes and behavior
K - 19. SHRINE	S. Exciting
D - 20. PETRIFY	T. Silent; unable to speak
F - 21. MEDICARE	U. Defrauding of money or property; swindling
P - 22. STUPOR	V. Feels sorry about
R - 23. PSYCHOLOGY	W. A state of abstract musing
H - 24. NAIVE	X. Hypnotized
N - 25. BLURTED	Y. Strong belief

Pigman's Legacy Vocabulary Matching 2

___ 1. NAIVE
___ 2. REGRETS
___ 3. INDIGENT
___ 4. WIDOW
___ 5. ZOMBIES
___ 6. PERKILY
___ 7. THROMBOSIS
___ 8. CONVENT
___ 9. GRUFF
___ 10. DOSSIER
___ 11. RHINESTONE
___ 12. GEOLOGY
___ 13. KEOGH
___ 14. INVERTED
___ 15. INSTINCTIVE
___ 16. STIMULATING
___ 17. STUPOR
___ 18. ANGUISH
___ 19. PSYCHOLOGY
___ 20. VIVACIOUSNESS
___ 21. WHEEZE
___ 22. APPARITION
___ 23. SURREPTITIOUSLY
___ 24. SUBMERGED
___ 25. ENGRAVED

A. A ghost
B. Feels sorry about
C. Retirement plan for the self-employed
D. Science of the origin, history and structure of the earth
E. Under; beneath
F. Turned inside out or up and down
G. Secretly
H. Formation of blood clot in a vessel or the heart
I. Liveliness; spiritedness; animation
J. Daze
K. People who look and behave like robots
L. Exciting
M. Science that deals with mental processes and behavior
N. In a lively way
O. A colorless artificial gem of paste or glass
P. Impulsive
Q. A monastic community or house, especially of nuns
R. Woman whose husband has died
S. Hoarse whistling sound
T. Brief and unfriendly; harsh
U. Simple; lacking in worldliness and sophistication
V. Collection of papers about a particular person
W. Impoverished; needy
X. Carved or etched into a surface
Y. Agonizing physical or mental pain

Pigman's Legacy Vocabulary Matching 2 Answer Key

U - 1. NAIVE		A. A ghost
B - 2. REGRETS		B. Feels sorry about
W - 3. INDIGENT		C. Retirement plan for the self-employed
R - 4. WIDOW		D. Science of the origin, history and structure of the earth
K - 5. ZOMBIES		E. Under; beneath
N - 6. PERKILY		F. Turned inside out or up and down
H - 7. THROMBOSIS		G. Secretly
Q - 8. CONVENT		H. Formation of blood clot in a vessel or the heart
T - 9. GRUFF		I. Liveliness; spiritedness; animation
V - 10. DOSSIER		J. Daze
O - 11. RHINESTONE		K. People who look and behave like robots
D - 12. GEOLOGY		L. Exciting
C - 13. KEOGH		M. Science that deals with mental processes and behavior
F - 14. INVERTED		N. In a lively way
P - 15. INSTINCTIVE		O. A colorless artificial gem of paste or glass
L - 16. STIMULATING		P. Impulsive
J - 17. STUPOR		Q. A monastic community or house, especially of nuns
Y - 18. ANGUISH		R. Woman whose husband has died
M - 19. PSYCHOLOGY		S. Hoarse whistling sound
I - 20. VIVACIOUSNESS		T. Brief and unfriendly; harsh
S - 21. WHEEZE		U. Simple; lacking in worldliness and sophistication
A - 22. APPARITION		V. Collection of papers about a particular person
G - 23. SURREPTITIOUSLY		W. Impoverished; needy
E - 24. SUBMERGED		X. Carved or etched into a surface
X - 25. ENGRAVED		Y. Agonizing physical or mental pain

Pigman's Legacy Vocabulary Matching 3

___ 1. CONVENT
___ 2. SQUATTING
___ 3. UNDULATING
___ 4. EPIC
___ 5. PSYCHOLOGY
___ 6. SURREPTITIOUSLY
___ 7. MORTIFIED
___ 8. BLURTED
___ 9. FLEECING
___ 10. TRESPASSING
___ 11. LEGACY
___ 12. VISION
___ 13. DILAPIDATED
___ 14. APPARITION
___ 15. PERKILY
___ 16. INSTINCTIVE
___ 17. MEDALLION
___ 18. DOSSIER
___ 19. ECSTASY
___ 20. GRAFFITI
___ 21. RHINESTONE
___ 22. MUTE
___ 23. VIVACIOUSNESS
___ 24. SUBMERGED
___ 25. SERENDIPITY

A. Something handed down, as from an ancestor
B. Invading the property rights of another
C. Defrauding of money or property; swindling
D. Collection of papers about a particular person
E. A ghost
F. In a lively way
G. In disrepair, deterioration, or ruin
H. Drawing or inscription on wall or other surface
I. Delight
J. Experience of seeing the supernatural as if with the eyes
K. A large medal
L. Silent; unable to speak
M. Making a wavelike movement
N. Literary work that suggests grandeur or heroics
O. Under; beneath
P. Said
Q. A colorless artificial gem of paste or glass
R. Settling without legal claim
S. Humiliated; shamed
T. Ability to make fortunate discoveries by accident
U. Liveliness; spiritedness; animation
V. Secretly
W. A monastic community or house, especially of nuns
X. Impulsive
Y. Science that deals with mental processes and behavior

Pigman's Legacy Vocabulary Matching 3 Answer Key

W - 1. CONVENT	A. Something handed down, as from an ancestor
R - 2. SQUATTING	B. Invading the property rights of another
M - 3. UNDULATING	C. Defrauding of money or property; swindling
N - 4. EPIC	D. Collection of papers about a particular person
Y - 5. PSYCHOLOGY	E. A ghost
V - 6. SURREPTITIOUSLY	F. In a lively way
S - 7. MORTIFIED	G. In disrepair, deterioration, or ruin
P - 8. BLURTED	H. Drawing or inscription on wall or other surface
C - 9. FLEECING	I. Delight
B - 10. TRESPASSING	J. Experience of seeing the supernatural as if with the eyes
A - 11. LEGACY	K. A large medal
J - 12. VISION	L. Silent; unable to speak
G - 13. DILAPIDATED	M. Making a wavelike movement
E - 14. APPARITION	N. Literary work that suggests grandeur or heroics
F - 15. PERKILY	O. Under; beneath
X - 16. INSTINCTIVE	P. Said
K - 17. MEDALLION	Q. A colorless artificial gem of paste or glass
D - 18. DOSSIER	R. Settling without legal claim
I - 19. ECSTASY	S. Humiliated; shamed
H - 20. GRAFFITI	T. Ability to make fortunate discoveries by accident
Q - 21. RHINESTONE	U. Liveliness; spiritedness; animation
L - 22. MUTE	V. Secretly
U - 23. VIVACIOUSNESS	W. A monastic community or house, especially of nuns
O - 24. SUBMERGED	X. Impulsive
T - 25. SERENDIPITY	Y. Science that deals with mental processes and behavior

Pigman's Legacy Vocabulary Matching 4

___ 1. WIDOW   A. Settling without legal claim
___ 2. INSTINCTIVE   B. Commemorating, serving as a reminder of
___ 3. DISCIPLE   C. Impulsive
___ 4. SURREPTITIOUSLY   D. Secretly
___ 5. VIVACIOUSNESS   E. A large medal
___ 6. MEMORIAL   F. Plants that purify crude substances
___ 7. REGRETS   G. Assistant; follower
___ 8. STEGOSAURUS   H. Delight
___ 9. FOIBLES   I. Defrauding of money or property; swindling
___10. REINCARNATED   J. Reborn
___11. DOSSIER   K. Science that deals with mental processes and behavior
___12. CONVICTION   L. Feels sorry about
___13. ABSTINENCE   M. Strong belief
___14. ECSTASY   N. Ability to make fortunate discoveries by accident
___15. ADOLESCENCE   O. Something handed down, as from an ancestor
___16. MEDALLION   P. Deliberate restraining of oneself; not indulging
___17. FLEECING   Q. Woman whose husband has died
___18. PSYCHOLOGY   R. Collection of papers about a particular person
___19. REFINERIES   S. Period from puberty to maturity; teen years
___20. SERENDIPITY   T. Hypnotized
___21. MESMERIZED   U. Minor weaknesses or failings of character
___22. ENGRAVED   V. Liveliness; spiritedness; animation
___23. MAUSOLEUM   W. A large stately tomb
___24. SQUATTING   X. Carved or etched into a surface
___25. LEGACY   Y. Dinosaur with a double row of bony plates on its back

Pigman's Legacy Vocabulary Matching 4 Answer Key

Q - 1. WIDOW		A. Settling without legal claim
C - 2. INSTINCTIVE		B. Commemorating, serving as a reminder of
G - 3. DISCIPLE		C. Impulsive
D - 4. SURREPTITIOUSLY		D. Secretly
V - 5. VIVACIOUSNESS		E. A large medal
B - 6. MEMORIAL		F. Plants that purify crude substances
L - 7. REGRETS		G. Assistant; follower
Y - 8. STEGOSAURUS		H. Delight
U - 9. FOIBLES		I. Defrauding of money or property; swindling
J - 10. REINCARNATED		J. Reborn
R - 11. DOSSIER		K. Science that deals with mental processes and behavior
M - 12. CONVICTION		L. Feels sorry about
P - 13. ABSTINENCE		M. Strong belief
H - 14. ECSTASY		N. Ability to make fortunate discoveries by accident
S - 15. ADOLESCENCE		O. Something handed down, as from an ancestor
E - 16. MEDALLION		P. Deliberate restraining of oneself; not indulging
I - 17. FLEECING		Q. Woman whose husband has died
K - 18. PSYCHOLOGY		R. Collection of papers about a particular person
F - 19. REFINERIES		S. Period from puberty to maturity; teen years
N - 20. SERENDIPITY		T. Hypnotized
T - 21. MESMERIZED		U. Minor weaknesses or failings of character
X - 22. ENGRAVED		V. Liveliness; spiritedness; animation
W - 23. MAUSOLEUM		W. A large stately tomb
A - 24. SQUATTING		X. Carved or etched into a surface
O - 25. LEGACY		Y. Dinosaur with a double row of bony plates on its back

Pigman's Legacy Vocabulary Magic Squares 1

Match the definition with the vocabulary word. Put your answers in the magic squares below. When your answers are correct, all columns and rows will add to the same number.

A. APPARITION
B. REGRETS
C. ANGUISH
D. STEGOSAURUS
E. SQUATTING
F. STIMULATING
G. MUTE
H. FLEECING
I. CONDONE
J. PLATONICALLY
K. ABSTINENCE
L. GRAFFITI
M. OMEN
N. GEOLOGY
O. SUBMERGED
P. DISCIPLE

1. Under; beneath
2. Transcending physical desire; spiritual
3. Defrauding of money or property; swindling
4. A ghost
5. Dinosaur with a double row of bony plates on its back
6. Settling without legal claim
7. Deliberate restraining of oneself; not indulging
8. Science of the origin, history and structure of the earth
9. Exciting
10. Agonizing physical or mental pain
11. Sigh of future good or evil
12. Drawing or inscription on wall or other surface
13. Overlook; forgive; disregard
14. Assistant; follower
15. Feels sorry about
16. Silent; unable to speak

A=	B=	C=	D=
E=	F=	G=	H=
I=	J=	K=	L=
M=	N=	O=	P=

Pigman's Legacy Vocabulary Magic Squares 1 Answer Key

Match the definition with the vocabulary word. Put your answers in the magic squares below. When your answers are correct, all columns and rows will add to the same number.

A. APPARITION
B. REGRETS
C. ANGUISH
D. STEGOSAURUS
E. SQUATTING
F. STIMULATING
G. MUTE
H. FLEECING
I. CONDONE
J. PLATONICALLY
K. ABSTINENCE
L. GRAFFITI
M. OMEN
N. GEOLOGY
O. SUBMERGED
P. DISCIPLE

1. Under; beneath
2. Transcending physical desire; spiritual
3. Defrauding of money or property; swindling
4. A ghost
5. Dinosaur with a double row of bony plates on its back
6. Settling without legal claim
7. Deliberate restraining of oneself; not indulging
8. Science of the origin, history and structure of the earth
9. Exciting
10. Agonizing physical or mental pain
11. Sigh of future good or evil
12. Drawing or inscription on wall or other surface
13. Overlook; forgive; disregard
14. Assistant; follower
15. Feels sorry about
16. Silent; unable to speak

A=4	B=15	C=10	D=5
E=6	F=9	G=16	H=3
I=13	J=2	K=7	L=12
M=11	N=8	O=1	P=14

Pigman's Legacy Vocabulary Magic Squares 2

Match the definition with the vocabulary word. Put your answers in the magic squares below. When your answers are correct, all columns and rows will add to the same number.

A. VIVACIOUSNESS
B. PSYCHOLOGY
C. MEDICARE
D. TRESPASSING
E. INDIGENT
F. STEGOSAURUS
G. PERKILY
H. DOSSIER
I. ADOLESCENCE
J. LEGACY
K. PLATONICALLY
L. UNDULATING
M. DISCIPLE
N. EPIC
O. REVERIE
P. IMMERSE

1. Government program for medical care for those over 65
2. Something handed down, as from an ancestor
3. Dinosaur with a double row of bony plates on its back
4. A state of abstract musing
5. Cover completely in something else
6. Impoverished; needy
7. Period from puberty to maturity; teen years
8. Invading the property rights of another
9. Assistant; follower
10. Collection of papers about a particular person
11. Making a wavelike movement
12. Liveliness; spiritedness; animation
13. Science that deals with mental processes and behavior
14. Transcending physical desire; spiritual
15. In a lively way
16. Literary work that suggests grandeur or heroics

A=	B=	C=	D=
E=	F=	G=	H=
I=	J=	K=	L=
M=	N=	O=	P=

Pigman's Legacy Vocabulary Magic Squares 2 Answer Key

Match the definition with the vocabulary word. Put your answers in the magic squares below. When your answers are correct, all columns and rows will add to the same number.

A. VIVACIOUSNESS
B. PSYCHOLOGY
C. MEDICARE
D. TRESPASSING
E. INDIGENT
F. STEGOSAURUS
G. PERKILY
H. DOSSIER
I. ADOLESCENCE
J. LEGACY
K. PLATONICALLY
L. UNDULATING
M. DISCIPLE
N. EPIC
O. REVERIE
P. IMMERSE

1. Government program for medical care for those over 65
2. Something handed down, as from an ancestor
3. Dinosaur with a double row of bony plates on its back
4. A state of abstract musing
5. Cover completely in something else
6. Impoverished; needy
7. Period from puberty to maturity; teen years
8. Invading the property rights of another
9. Assistant; follower
10. Collection of papers about a particular person
11. Making a wavelike movement
12. Liveliness; spiritedness; animation
13. Science that deals with mental processes and behavior
14. Transcending physical desire; spiritual
15. In a lively way
16. Literary work that suggests grandeur or heroics

A=12	B=13	C=1	D=8
E=6	F=3	G=15	H=10
I=7	J=2	K=14	L=11
M=9	N=16	O=4	P=5

Pigman's Legacy Vocabulary Magic Squares 3

Match the definition with the vocabulary word. Put your answers in the magic squares below. When your answers are correct, all columns and rows will add to the same number.

A. SURREPTITIOUSLY
B. OMEN
C. INDIGENT
D. ZOMBIES
E. UNDULATING
F. REINCARNATED
G. MANNEQUINS
H. PSYCHOLOGY
I. REFINERIES
J. GRUFF
K. EPIC
L. MORTIFIED
M. SHRINE
N. MEMORIAL
O. REVERIE
P. FOIBLES

1. Impoverished; needy
2. Brief and unfriendly; harsh
3. Reborn
4. A state of abstract musing
5. Minor weaknesses or failings of character
6. Making a wavelike movement
7. Plants that purify crude substances
8. People who look and behave like robots
9. Site revered for its associations
10. Science that deals with mental processes and behavior
11. Humiliated; shamed
12. Secretly
13. Sigh of future good or evil
14. Literary work that suggests grandeur or heroics
15. Dummies
16. Commemorating, serving as a reminder of

A=	B=	C=	D=
E=	F=	G=	H=
I=	J=	K=	L=
M=	N=	O=	P=

Pigman's Legacy Vocabulary Magic Squares 3 Answer Key

Match the definition with the vocabulary word. Put your answers in the magic squares below. When your answers are correct, all columns and rows will add to the same number.

A. SURREPTITIOUSLY
B. OMEN
C. INDIGENT
D. ZOMBIES
E. UNDULATING
F. REINCARNATED
G. MANNEQUINS
H. PSYCHOLOGY
I. REFINERIES
J. GRUFF
K. EPIC
L. MORTIFIED
M. SHRINE
N. MEMORIAL
O. REVERIE
P. FOIBLES

1. Impoverished; needy
2. Brief and unfriendly; harsh
3. Reborn
4. A state of abstract musing
5. Minor weaknesses or failings of character
6. Making a wavelike movement
7. Plants that purify crude substances
8. People who look and behave like robots
9. Site revered for its associations
10. Science that deals with mental processes and behavior
11. Humiliated; shamed
12. Secretly
13. Sigh of future good or evil
14. Literary work that suggests grandeur or heroics
15. Dummies
16. Commemorating, serving as a reminder of

A=12	B=13	C=1	D=8
E=6	F=3	G=15	H=10
I=7	J=2	K=14	L=11
M=9	N=16	O=4	P=5

Pigman's Legacy Vocabulary Magic Squares 4

Match the definition with the vocabulary word. Put your answers in the magic squares below. When your answers are correct, all columns and rows will add to the same number.

A. APPARITION
B. MESMERIZED
C. SQUATTING
D. PSYCHOLOGY
E. CONVICTION
F. PUBESCENT
G. CONDONE
H. FLEECING
I. LEGACY
J. MEDICARE
K. STUPOR
L. GRUFF
M. BLURTED
N. INDIGENT
O. ADOLESCENCE
P. TRESPASSING

1. Defrauding of money or property; swindling
2. A ghost
3. Hypnotized
4. Overlook; forgive; disregard
5. Government program for medical care for those over 65
6. Period from puberty to maturity; teen years
7. Invading the property rights of another
8. Something handed down, as from an ancestor
9. Daze
10. Impoverished; needy
11. Said
12. Brief and unfriendly; harsh
13. Strong belief
14. Science that deals with mental processes and behavior
15. Settling without legal claim
16. Reaching or having reached puberty

A= 2	B= 3	C= 15	D= 14
E= 13	F= 16	G= 4	H= 1
I= 8	J= 5	K= 9	L= 12
M= 11	N= 10	O= 6	P= 7

Pigman's Legacy Vocabulary Magic Squares 4 Answer Key

Match the definition with the vocabulary word. Put your answers in the magic squares below. When your answers are correct, all columns and rows will add to the same number.

A. APPARITION
B. MESMERIZED
C. SQUATTING
D. PSYCHOLOGY
E. CONVICTION
F. PUBESCENT
G. CONDONE
H. FLEECING
I. LEGACY
J. MEDICARE
K. STUPOR
L. GRUFF
M. BLURTED
N. INDIGENT
O. ADOLESCENCE
P. TRESPASSING

1. Defrauding of money or property; swindling
2. A ghost
3. Hypnotized
4. Overlook; forgive; disregard
5. Government program for medical care for those over 65
6. Period from puberty to maturity; teen years
7. Invading the property rights of another
8. Something handed down, as from an ancestor
9. Daze
10. Impoverished; needy
11. Said
12. Brief and unfriendly; harsh
13. Strong belief
14. Science that deals with mental processes and behavior
15. Settling without legal claim
16. Reaching or having reached puberty

A=2	B=3	C=15	D=14
E=13	F=16	G=4	H=1
I=8	J=5	K=9	L=12
M=11	N=10	O=6	P=7

Pigman's Legacy Vocabulary Word Search 1

```
M A N N E Q U I N S M K E O G H Q K N L
D O S S I E R R D Z O M B I E S Y B O I
Y T F L N H D E V A R G N E P S F L I M
S V L W V X Y N T X T V V D A C L U T I
V U H G E O L O G Y I T J T W J E R C T
S J R V R H L D O S F T S E P F E T I A
S C Q R T H C N I M I C V C L Z C E V T
R H I N E S T O N E E H T N E G I D N I
E J R T D P N C N P D N Y E V P N X O O
F A U I S I T Z Y V D W F N S U G Y C N
I M P V N Z L I L E E I I I M B Y M H S
N N E P C E G A T S T N R T L E G A C Y
E A I G A S I I P I T P T S E S O U I H
R I R S M R N G F I O U E B P C L S M F
I V E T O G I F R O D U P A I E O O M D
E E V M I W A T A U S A S O C N H L E G
S F E V Y R I F I B F S T L R T C E R K
B M R K G T H D L O J F I E Y N Y U S M
M E D I C A R E O R N J S L D R S M E Q
F O I B L E S Q X W H E E Z E B P H N M
```

A colorless artificial gem of paste or glass (10)
A ghost (10)
A large stately tomb (9)
A monastic community or house, especially of nuns (7)
A state of abstract musing (7)
Brief and unfriendly; harsh (5)
Carved or etched into a surface (8)
Collection of papers about a particular person (7)
Come to become stonelike; to deaden (7)
Commemorating, serving as a reminder of (8)
Cover completely in something else (7)
Daze (6)
Defrauding of money or property; swindling (8)
Deliberate restraining of oneself; not indulging (10)
Delight (7)
Drawing or inscription on wall or other surface (8)
Dummies (10)
Experience of seeing the supernatural as if with the eyes (6)
Government program for medical care for those over 65 (8)
Hoarse whistling sound (6)
Humiliated; shamed (9)
Impoverished; needy (8)
In disrepair, deterioration, or ruin (11)
Lit up (7)
Literary work that suggests grandeur or heroics (4)
Minor weaknesses or failings of character (7)
Not substantial; slight (5)
Overlook; forgive; disregard (7)
People who look and behave like robots (7)
Plants that purify crude substances (10)
Reaching or having reached puberty (9)
Restrictions; boundaries (11)
Retirement plan for the self-employed (5)
Said (7)
Science of the origin, history and structure of the earth (7)
Science that deals with mental processes and behavior (10)
Secretly (15)
Sigh of future good or evil (4)
Silent; unable to speak (4)
Simple; lacking in worldliness and sophistication (5)
Site revered for its associations (6)
Skeleton or leaf imprint (6)
Something handed down, as from an ancestor (6)
Strong belief (10)
Turned inside out or up and down (8)
Woman whose husband has died (5)

Pigman's Legacy Vocabulary Word Search 1 Answer Key

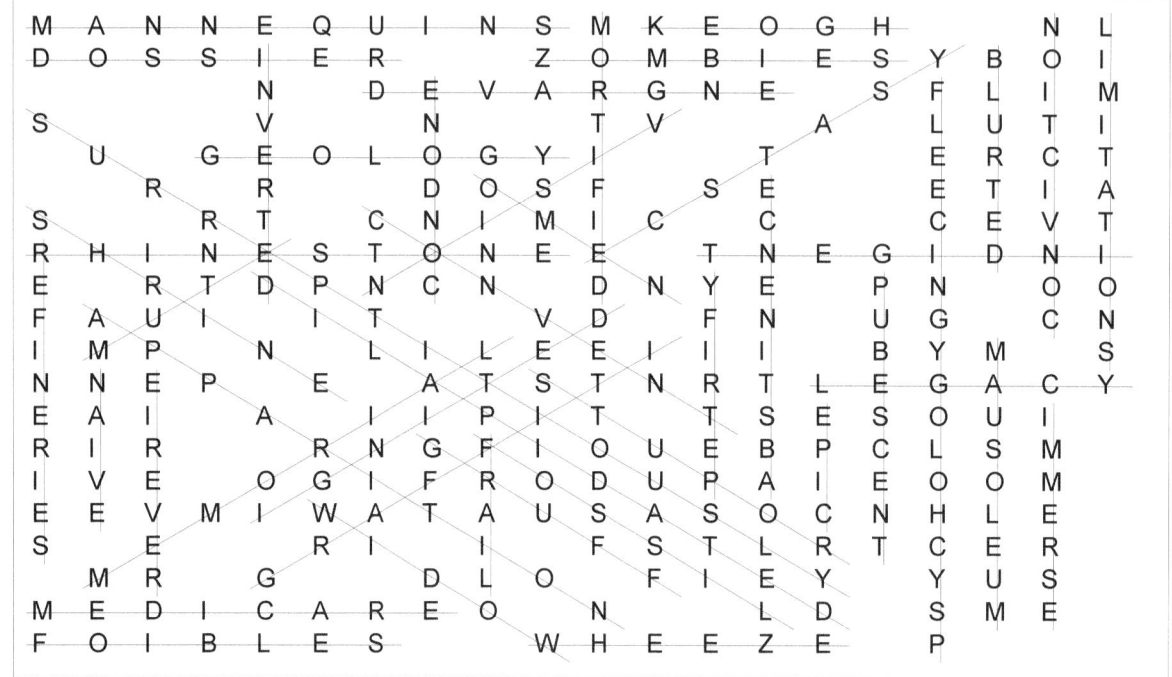

A colorless artificial gem of paste or glass (10)
A ghost (10)
A large stately tomb (9)
A monastic community or house, especially of nuns (7)
A state of abstract musing (7)
Brief and unfriendly; harsh (5)
Carved or etched into a surface (8)
Collection of papers about a particular person (7)
Come to become stonelike; to deaden (7)
Commemorating, serving as a reminder of (8)
Cover completely in something else (7)
Daze (6)
Defrauding of money or property; swindling (8)
Deliberate restraining of oneself; not indulging (10)
Delight (7)
Drawing or inscription on wall or other surface (8)
Dummies (10)
Experience of seeing the supernatural as if with the eyes (6)
Government program for medical care for those over 65 (8)
Hoarse whistling sound (6)
Humiliated; shamed (9)
Impoverished; needy (8)
In disrepair, deterioration, or ruin (11)
Lit up (7)

Literary work that suggests grandeur or heroics (4)
Minor weaknesses or failings of character (7)
Not substantial; slight (5)
Overlook; forgive; disregard (7)
People who look and behave like robots (7)
Plants that purify crude substances (10)
Reaching or having reached puberty (9)
Restrictions; boundaries (11)
Retirement plan for the self-employed (5)
Said (7)
Science of the origin, history and structure of the earth (7)
Science that deals with mental processes and behavior (10)
Secretly (15)
Sigh of future good or evil (4)
Silent; unable to speak (4)
Simple; lacking in worldliness and sophistication (5)
Site revered for its associations (6)
Skeleton or leaf imprint (6)
Something handed down, as from an ancestor (6)
Strong belief (10)
Turned inside out or up and down (8)
Woman whose husband has died (5)

Pigman's Legacy Vocabulary Word Search 2

```
P R E G R E T S I S O B M O R H T C S D
S F D L X G P T G L E G A C Y G P J U B
Y O Y I W N E U R H X X W D R S T R B F
C I T S S I R P U B E S C E N T W B M M
H B I S R C K O F Y E Q I I N E A L E W
O L P O P E I R F V T N W F A G N I R P
L E I F A E L P I G C J G I P O G M G C
O S D B B L Y T L A R S W T P S U I E B
G V N L S F C R R E X G L R A A I T D T
Y I E U T N Q N F R A I L O R U S A E F
S S R R I M A U S O L E U M I R H T C B
H I E T N T F G E M G N E B T U R I S Q
R O S E E Z L P P N L D N Z I S I O T Y
E N O D N O C E I M A W I D O W N N A V
I B A Y C Y V T C L I H P M N M E S S B
S V M I E S T R L Y R E Y K M V B W Y J
S B U B V A Y I Z W O E D E N E O I L L
O Q T Z U E O F K Z M Z W O Y D R M E P
D J E Q C N T Y D Q E E C G L M X S E S
M E S M E R I Z E D M H V H J H Y T E N
```

A ghost (10)
A large medal (9)
A large stately tomb (9)
A monastic community or house, especially of nuns (7)
Ability to make fortunate discoveries by accident (11)
Agonizing physical or mental pain (7)
Assistant; follower (8)
Brief and unfriendly; harsh (5)
Collection of papers about a particular person (7)
Come to become stonelike; to deaden (7)
Commemorating, serving as a reminder of (8)
Cover completely in something else (7)
Daze (6)
Defrauding of money or property; swindling (8)
Deliberate restraining of oneself; not indulging (10)
Delight (7)
Dinosaur with a double row of bony plates on its back (11)
Experience of seeing the supernatural as if with the eyes (6)
Feels sorry about (7)
Formation of blood clot in a vessel or the heart (10)
Hoarse whistling sound (6)
Humiliated; shamed (9)

Hypnotized (10)
Impulsive (11)
In a lively way (7)
Literary work that suggests grandeur or heroics (4)
Minor weaknesses or failings of character (7)
Not substantial; slight (5)
Overlook; forgive; disregard (7)
People who look and behave like robots (7)
Reaching or having reached puberty (9)
Reborn (12)
Restrictions; boundaries (11)
Retirement plan for the self-employed (5)
Said (7)
Science that deals with mental processes and behavior (10)
Settling without legal claim (9)
Sigh of future good or evil (4)
Silent; unable to speak (4)
Simple; lacking in worldliness and sophistication (5)
Site revered for its associations (6)
Skeleton or leaf imprint (6)
Something handed down, as from an ancestor (6)
Under; beneath (9)
Woman whose husband has died (5)

Pigman's Legacy Vocabulary Word Search 2 Answer Key

A ghost (10)
A large medal (9)
A large stately tomb (9)
A monastic community or house, especially of nuns (7)
Ability to make fortunate discoveries by accident (11)
Agonizing physical or mental pain (7)
Assistant; follower (8)
Brief and unfriendly; harsh (5)
Collection of papers about a particular person (7)
Come to become stonelike; to deaden (7)
Commemorating, serving as a reminder of (8)
Cover completely in something else (7)
Daze (6)
Defrauding of money or property; swindling (8)
Deliberate restraining of oneself; not indulging (10)
Delight (7)
Dinosaur with a double row of bony plates on its back (11)
Experience of seeing the supernatural as if with the eyes (6)
Feels sorry about (7)
Formation of blood clot in a vessel or the heart (10)
Hoarse whistling sound (6)
Humiliated; shamed (9)

Hypnotized (10)
Impulsive (11)
In a lively way (7)
Literary work that suggests grandeur or heroics (4)
Minor weaknesses or failings of character (7)
Not substantial; slight (5)
Overlook; forgive; disregard (7)
People who look and behave like robots (7)
Reaching or having reached puberty (9)
Reborn (12)
Restrictions; boundaries (11)
Retirement plan for the self-employed (5)
Said (7)
Science that deals with mental processes and behavior (10)
Settling without legal claim (9)
Sigh of future good or evil (4)
Silent; unable to speak (4)
Simple; lacking in worldliness and sophistication (5)
Site revered for its associations (6)
Skeleton or leaf imprint (6)
Something handed down, as from an ancestor (6)
Under; beneath (9)
Woman whose husband has died (5)

Pigman's Legacy Vocabulary Word Search 3

```
A F R A I L M G N I S S A P S E R T S F
N M G Z N F J A N F N G F P L V N M U Q
G B E Y O B O V N N O D R P H I O H R Z
U L H S H M E I O N S S I U M A I M R Z
I U D E M R B I B L E C S G F N S H E L
S R N R T E L I W L S Q C I E F I D P M
H T B E W L R R E I E X U W L N V E T Z
S E D N A Q C I D S F S Y I E W T T I Y
H D M D G I O S Z R C S R S N P I A T T
P G E I E N N B N E A T T Q T S F D I N
B M D P O S D J L T D O K Y T V L I O Q
G C I I L T O S S V N G P K M G E P U W
B R C T O I N C R E V E R I E Q E A S Z
S R A Y G N E P K L I W J D M S C L L C
T R R F Y C E Y N G D L O J O H I I Y C
U X E X F T W P N E W S I B R R N D O Q
P W W G R I W I V T S X M Q I I G N N N
O R V I R V T A V I L X M Q A N V M H S
R E F I N E R I E S O M E N L E G A C Y
R Y M J D G T R L H U P R M N K E O G H
V W C X N G X S R T I B S T W P L D K R
W H E E Z E W W E C M U E L O S U A M G
```

ANGUISH
BLURTED
CONDONE
CONVENT
DILAPIDATED
DISCIPLE
DOSSIER
ECSTASY
ENGRAVED
EPIC
FLEECING
FOIBLES

FOSSIL
FRAIL
GEOLOGY
GRAFFITI
GRUFF
IGNITED
IMMERSE
INDIGENT
INSTINCTIVE
INVERTED
KEOGH
LEGACY

MANNEQUINS
MAUSOLEUM
MEDALLION
MEDICARE
MEMORIAL
MESMERIZED
MUTE
NAIVE
OMEN
PETRIFY
REFINERIES
REGRETS

REVERIE
RHINESTONE
SERENDIPITY
SHRINE
STUPOR
SURREPTITIOUSLY
TRESPASSING
VISION
WHEEZE
WIDOW
ZOMBIES

Pigman's Legacy Vocabulary Word Search 3 Answer Key

ANGUISH	FOSSIL	MANNEQUINS	REVERIE
BLURTED	FRAIL	MAUSOLEUM	RHINESTONE
CONDONE	GEOLOGY	MEDALLION	SERENDIPITY
CONVENT	GRAFFITI	MEDICARE	SHRINE
DILAPIDATED	GRUFF	MEMORIAL	STUPOR
DISCIPLE	IGNITED	MESMERIZED	SURREPTITIOUSLY
DOSSIER	IMMERSE	MUTE	TRESPASSING
ECSTASY	INDIGENT	NAIVE	VISION
ENGRAVED	INSTINCTIVE	OMEN	WHEEZE
EPIC	INVERTED	PETRIFY	WIDOW
FLEECING	KEOGH	REFINERIES	ZOMBIES
FOIBLES	LEGACY	REGRETS	

Pigman's Legacy Vocabulary Word Search 4

```
K C O N V E N T F O I B L E S L E P I C
Z E W K M Z N H L C Z O M B I E S V N Y
W L O M L E D H E O R K P X W G P I V T
K Y W G G N E X E N V E T S Y A U S E K
F W P I H X T J C V C L V L C C B I R G
W X D E Z S I J I I X G S E B Y E O T V
A N B R T V N T N C R U B Q R X S N E L
I P B U H R G G G T O P P R H I C D D R
E L P I C S I D L I N S T E R G E R P J
M O K A X P K F T O R N C D X T N B E M
R L W Z R W S I Y N E S S P A S T K R F
N N D N H I T W B M T G H N N T G V K H
F R A I L P T R O A T H R O M B O S I S
W F L I E V E I S Y S A I U Q N U T L W
M J D R V I B Y O I C T N S F B I H Y N
J E R B S E Y W U N A R E Q M F D E L B
W U D S L G S G I T M U T E F O S S I L
S I O I O U N E I H R V R A R Z K R X M
L D D L C A R M D Z Q G R J W H E E Z E
L T O O Y A I T Z S E G L A I R O M E M
Y E V Z W L R V E D C O N D O N E M F J
G E N G R A V E D D U N D U L A T I N G
```

ANGUISH	FOIBLES	LIMITATIONS	SHRINE
APPARITION	FOSSIL	MEDICARE	STUPOR
BLURTED	FRAIL	MEMORIAL	SUBMERGED
CONDONE	GEOLOGY	MUTE	SURREPTITIOUSLY
CONVENT	GRAFFITI	NAIVE	THROMBOSIS
CONVICTION	GRUFF	OMEN	UNDULATING
DISCIPLE	IGNITED	PERKILY	VISION
DOSSIER	IMMERSE	PETRIFY	WHEEZE
ECSTASY	INDIGENT	PUBESCENT	WIDOW
ENGRAVED	INVERTED	REGRETS	ZOMBIES
EPIC	KEOGH	REINCARNATED	
FLEECING	LEGACY	REVERIE	

Pigman's Legacy Vocabulary Word Search 4 Answer Key

```
K C O N V E N T F O I B L E S L E P I C
  E         N       L C Z O M B I E S V N
    O     E D     E O R       G P I V E
      G G   E     E N     E     Y A U S R
    P I H   T     C   E   V L     C B I T
    D E     S     I   I   S E     Y E O E
A   N       T     N   C   U       R   S N D
I   P   U   R G   G   T O         R   I C D
E L P I C S I D   I     S T E R G E R P
    O   A     F T O     N C         N   E
R       R     I Y N E S S   A   S   T   R
    N         I   M T G H N N           K
  F R A I L P T R O A T H R O M B O S I S
      I     E   E I S   S A I U   U T   L
  M     R V I     Y O I C T N   F B I   Y
    E R B S E Y   U N A   E     M F   E
  W U D S L G   G I T   M U T E F O S S I L
  S I O I O U N E I       R A         R
      D D L C A R M       G R   W H E E Z E
        O O   A I T     E G L A I R O M E M
      E     W L R   E D C O N D O N E M
    G E N G R A V E D D U N D U L A T I N G
```

ANGUISH	FOIBLES	LIMITATIONS	SHRINE
APPARITION	FOSSIL	MEDICARE	STUPOR
BLURTED	FRAIL	MEMORIAL	SUBMERGED
CONDONE	GEOLOGY	MUTE	SURREPTITIOUSLY
CONVENT	GRAFFITI	NAIVE	THROMBOSIS
CONVICTION	GRUFF	OMEN	UNDULATING
DISCIPLE	IGNITED	PERKILY	VISION
DOSSIER	IMMERSE	PETRIFY	WHEEZE
ECSTASY	INDIGENT	PUBESCENT	WIDOW
ENGRAVED	INVERTED	REGRETS	ZOMBIES
EPIC	KEOGH	REINCARNATED	
FLEECING	LEGACY	REVERIE	

Pigman's Legacy Vocabulary Crossword 1

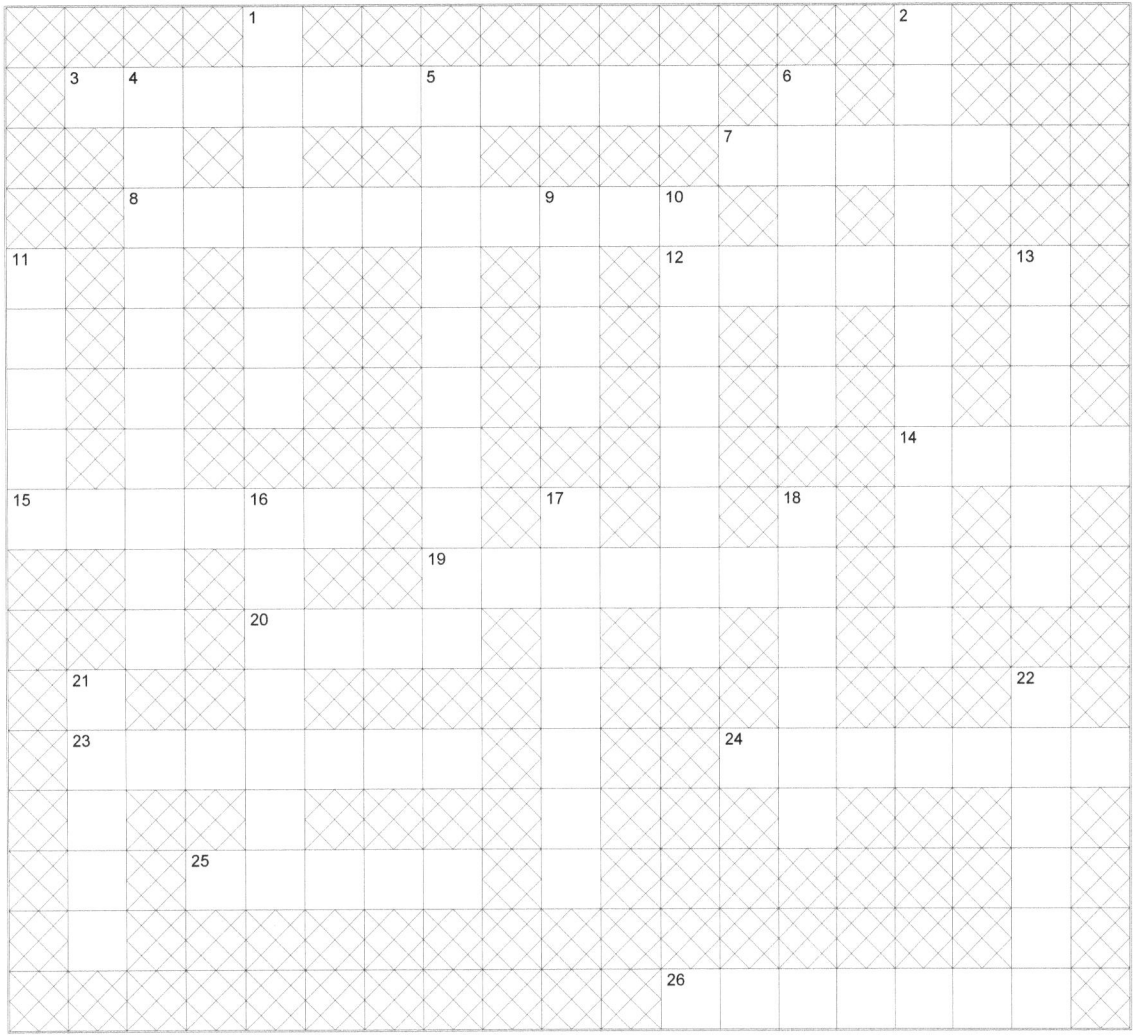

Across
3. Dinosaur with a double row of bony plates on its back
7. Woman whose husband has died
8. A colorless artificial gem of paste or glass
12. Simple; lacking in worldliness and sophistication
14. Literary work that suggests grandeur or heroics
15. Skeleton or leaf imprint
19. A monastic community or house, especially of nuns
20. Silent; unable to speak
23. Feels sorry about
24. Minor weaknesses or failings of character
25. Retirement plan for the self-employed
26. In a lively way

Down
1. Lit up
2. Period from puberty to maturity; teen years
4. Formation of blood clot in a vessel or the heart
5. Deliberate restraining of oneself; not indulging
6. Experience of seeing the supernatural as if with the eyes
9. Sigh of future good or evil
10. Carved or etched into a surface
11. Brief and unfriendly; harsh
13. Site revered for its associations
16. Cover completely in something else
17. Agonizing physical or mental pain
18. Daze
21. Not substantial; slight
22. Something handed down, as from an ancestor

Pigman's Legacy Vocabulary Crossword 1 Answer Key

Across

3. Dinosaur with a double row of bony plates on its back
7. Woman whose husband has died
8. A colorless artificial gem of paste or glass
12. Simple; lacking in worldliness and sophistication
14. Literary work that suggests grandeur or heroics
15. Skeleton or leaf imprint
19. A monastic community or house, especially of nuns
20. Silent; unable to speak
23. Feels sorry about
24. Minor weaknesses or failings of character
25. Retirement plan for the self-employed
26. In a lively way

Down

1. Lit up
2. Period from puberty to maturity; teen years
4. Formation of blood clot in a vessel or the heart
5. Deliberate restraining of oneself; not indulging
6. Experience of seeing the supernatural as if with the eyes
9. Sigh of future good or evil
10. Carved or etched into a surface
11. Brief and unfriendly; harsh
13. Site revered for its associations
16. Cover completely in something else
17. Agonizing physical or mental pain
18. Daze
21. Not substantial; slight
22. Something handed down, as from an ancestor

Pigman's Legacy Vocabulary Crossword 2

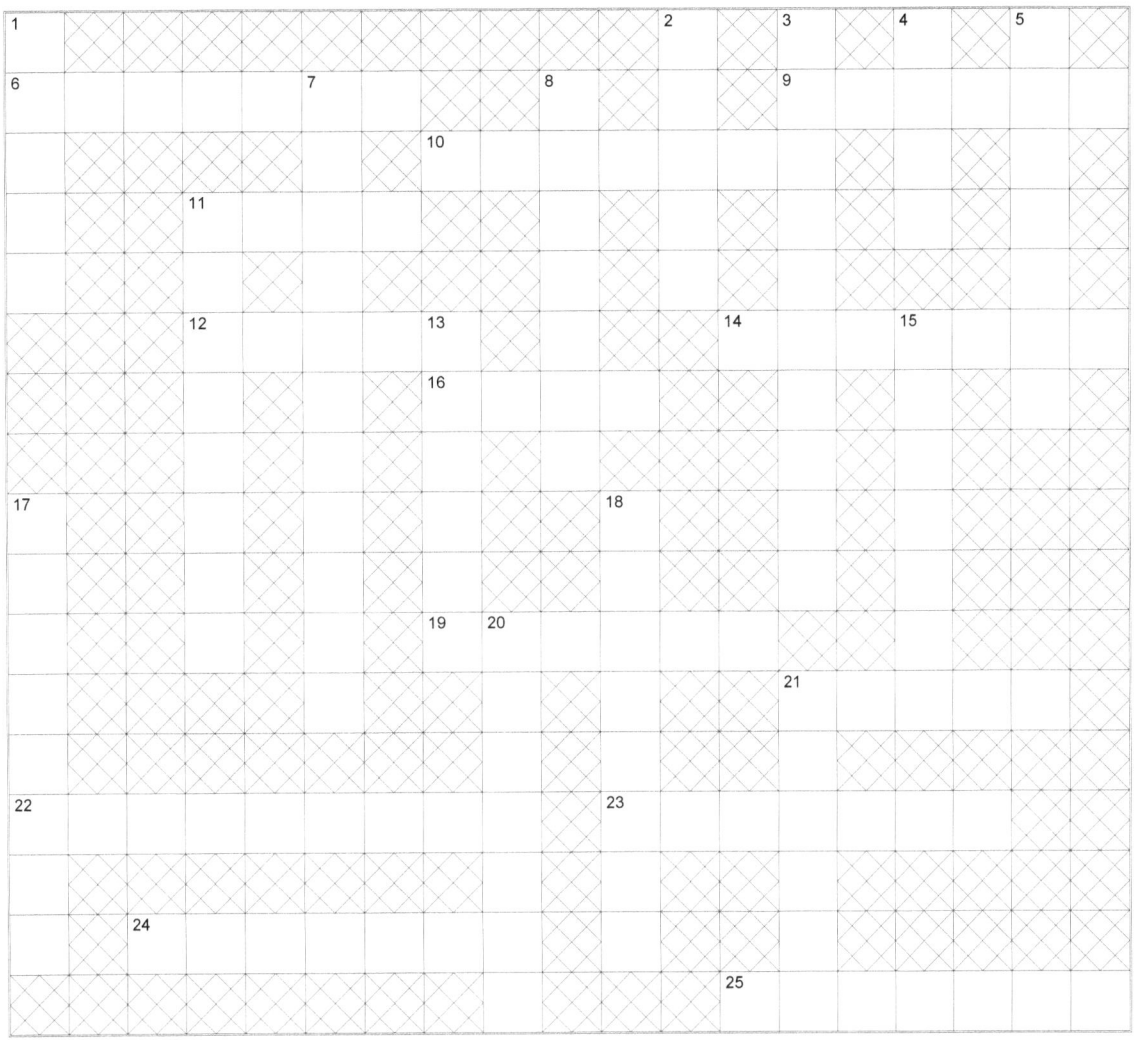

Across
6. Agonizing physical or mental pain
9. Daze
10. Science of the origin, history and structure of the earth
11. Literary work that suggests grandeur or heroics
12. Brief and unfriendly; harsh
14. Minor weaknesses or failings of character
16. Sigh of future good or evil
19. Something handed down, as from an ancestor
21. Woman whose husband has died
22. Reaching or having reached puberty
23. Cover completely in something else
24. Feels sorry about
25. In a lively way

Down
1. Simple; lacking in worldliness and sophistication
2. Retirement plan for the self-employed
3. Science that deals with mental processes and behavior
4. Silent; unable to speak
5. Collection of papers about a particular person
7. Exciting
8. People who look and behave like robots
11. Carved or etched into a surface
13. Skeleton or leaf imprint
15. Said
17. Assistant; follower
18. Drawing or inscription on wall or other surface
20. Delight
21. Hoarse whistling sound

Pigman's Legacy Vocabulary Crossword 2 Answer Key

Across
6. Agonizing physical or mental pain
9. Daze
10. Science of the origin, history and structure of the earth
11. Literary work that suggests grandeur or heroics
12. Brief and unfriendly; harsh
14. Minor weaknesses or failings of character
16. Sigh of future good or evil
19. Something handed down, as from an ancestor
21. Woman whose husband has died
22. Reaching or having reached puberty
23. Cover completely in something else
24. Feels sorry about
25. In a lively way

Down
1. Simple; lacking in worldliness and sophistication
2. Retirement plan for the self-employed
3. Science that deals with mental processes and behavior
4. Silent; unable to speak
5. Collection of papers about a particular person
7. Exciting
8. People who look and behave like robots
11. Carved or etched into a surface
13. Skeleton or leaf imprint
15. Said
17. Assistant; follower
18. Drawing or inscription on wall or other surface
20. Delight
21. Hoarse whistling sound

Pigman's Legacy Vocabulary Crossword 3

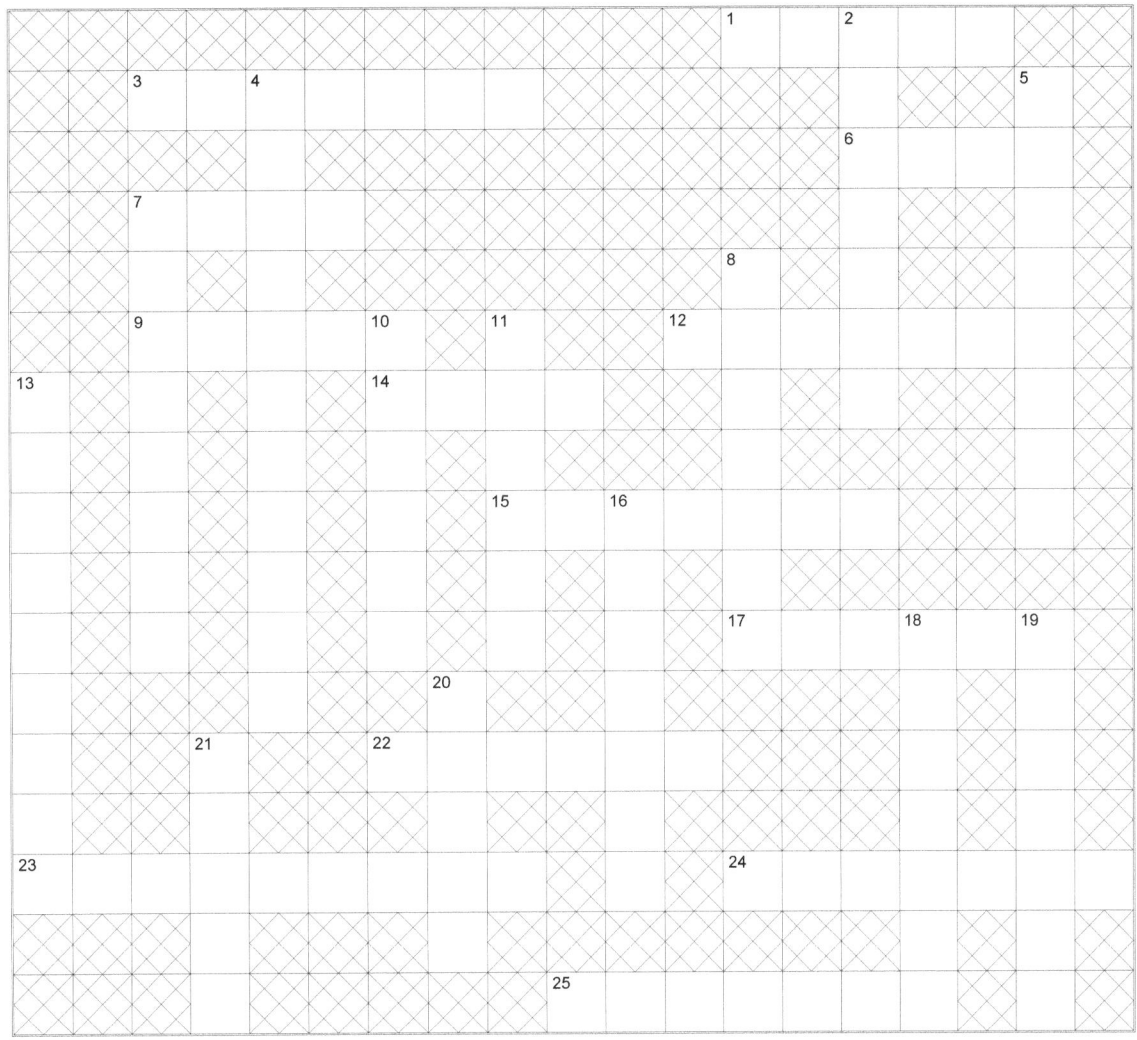

Across
1. Simple; lacking in worldliness and sophistication
3. Delight
6. Silent; unable to speak
7. Literary work that suggests grandeur or heroics
9. Brief and unfriendly; harsh
12. Collection of papers about a particular person
14. Sigh of future good or evil
15. Agonizing physical or mental pain
17. Daze
22. Experience of seeing the supernatural as if with the eyes
23. A large medal
24. Lit up
25. Come to become stonelike; to deaden

Down
2. Cover completely in something else
4. Exciting
5. Commemorating, serving as a reminder of
7. Carved or etched into a surface
8. People who look and behave like robots
10. Skeleton or leaf imprint
11. Something handed down, as from an ancestor
13. A large stately tomb
16. Science of the origin, history and structure of the earth
18. In a lively way
19. Feels sorry about
20. Woman whose husband has died
21. Not substantial; slight

Pigman's Legacy Vocabulary Crossword 3 Answer Key

Across
1. Simple; lacking in worldliness and sophistication
3. Delight
6. Silent; unable to speak
7. Literary work that suggests grandeur or heroics
9. Brief and unfriendly; harsh
12. Collection of papers about a particular person
14. Sigh of future good or evil
15. Agonizing physical or mental pain
17. Daze
22. Experience of seeing the supernatural as if with the eyes
23. A large medal
24. Lit up
25. Come to become stonelike; to deaden

Down
2. Cover completely in something else
4. Exciting
5. Commemorating, serving as a reminder of
7. Carved or etched into a surface
8. People who look and behave like robots
10. Skeleton or leaf imprint
11. Something handed down, as from an ancestor
13. A large stately tomb
16. Science of the origin, history and structure of the earth
18. In a lively way
19. Feels sorry about
20. Woman whose husband has died
21. Not substantial; slight

Pigman's Legacy Vocabulary Crossword 4

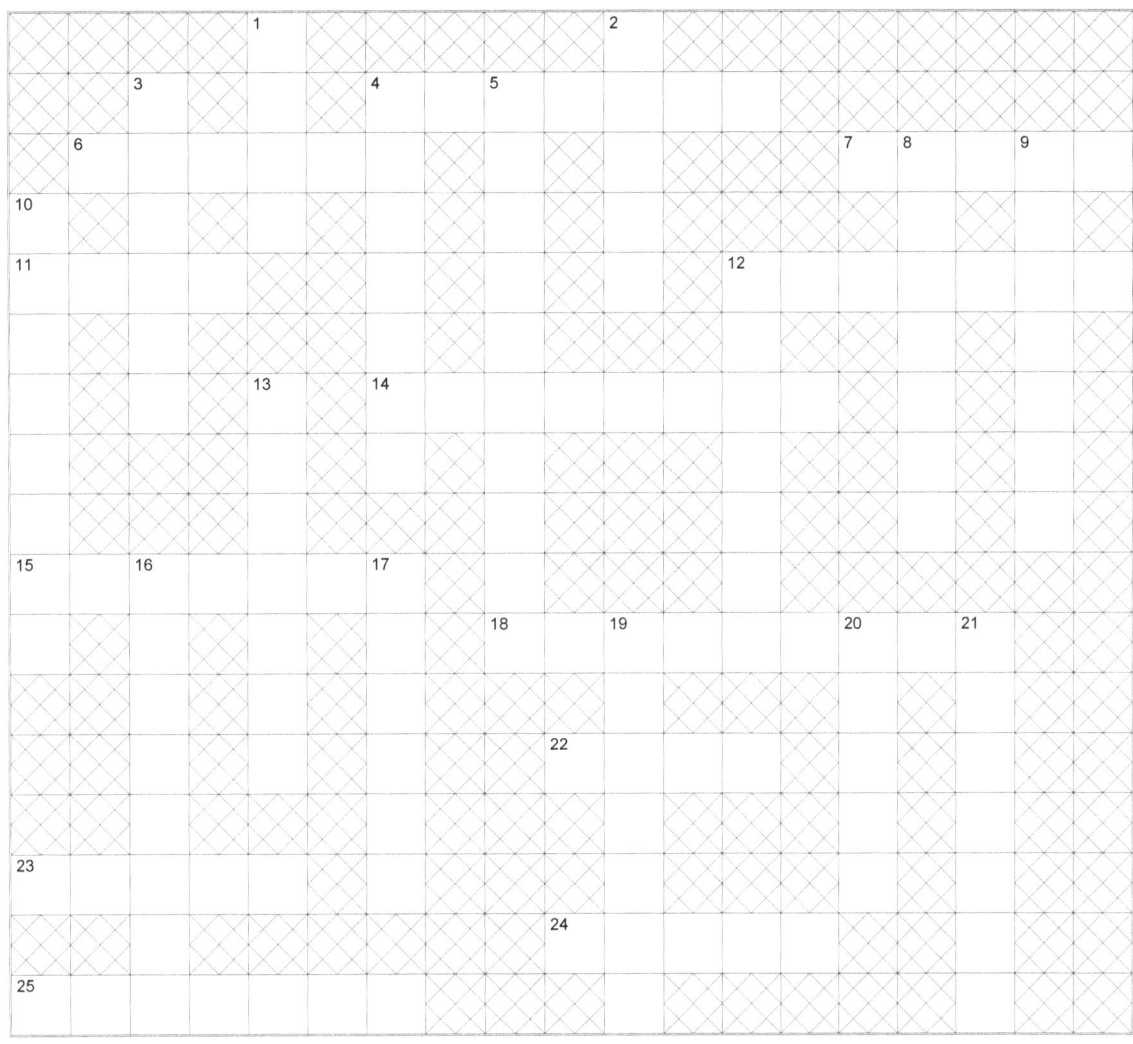

Across
4. In a lively way
6. Hoarse whistling sound
7. Not substantial; slight
11. Literary work that suggests grandeur or heroics
12. A monastic community or house, especially of nuns
14. Defrauding of money or property; swindling
15. Feels sorry about
18. Under; beneath
22. Silent; unable to speak
23. Simple; lacking in worldliness and sophistication
24. Retirement plan for the self-employed
25. Minor weaknesses or failings of character

Down
1. Sigh of future good or evil
2. Woman whose husband has died
3. Site revered for its associations
4. Come to become stonelike; to deaden
5. Plants that purify crude substances
8. A state of abstract musing
9. Lit up
10. Government program for medical care for those over 65
12. Overlook; forgive; disregard
13. Cover completely in something else
16. Drawing or inscription on wall or other surface
17. Daze
19. Said
20. Brief and unfriendly; harsh
21. Collection of papers about a particular person

Pigman's Legacy Vocabulary Crossword 4 Answer Key

				¹O				²W				
		³S		M	⁴P	E	⁵R	K	¹I	L	Y	
	⁶W	H	E	E	Z	E		E		D		⁷F	⁸R	⁹A	I	L
¹⁰M		R		N		T		F		O			E		G	
¹¹E	P	I	C			R		I		W		¹²C	O	N	V	E	N	T
D		N				I		N		O			E		I	
I		E		¹³I	¹⁴F	L	E	E	C	I	N	G		R		T
C				M		Y		R				D		I		E
A				M				I				O		E		D
¹⁵R	E	¹⁶G	R	E	T	¹⁷S		E				N				
E		R		R		T		¹⁸S	U	¹⁹B	M	E	R	²⁰G	²¹E	D
		A		S		U				L				R		O
		F		E		P		²²M	U	T	E			U		S
		F				O				R				F		S
²³N	A	I	V	E		R				T				F		I
		T						²⁴K	E	O	G	H				E
²⁵F	O	I	B	L	E	S		D								R

Across
4. In a lively way
6. Hoarse whistling sound
7. Not substantial; slight
11. Literary work that suggests grandeur or heroics
12. A monastic community or house, especially of nuns
14. Defrauding of money or property; swindling
15. Feels sorry about
18. Under; beneath
22. Silent; unable to speak
23. Simple; lacking in worldliness and sophistication
24. Retirement plan for the self-employed
25. Minor weaknesses or failings of character

Down
1. Sigh of future good or evil
2. Woman whose husband has died
3. Site revered for its associations
4. Come to become stonelike; to deaden
5. Plants that purify crude substances
8. A state of abstract musing
9. Lit up
10. Government program for medical care for those over 65
12. Overlook; forgive; disregard
13. Cover completely in something else
16. Drawing or inscription on wall or other surface
17. Daze
19. Said
20. Brief and unfriendly; harsh
21. Collection of papers about a particular person

Pigman's Legacy Vocabulary Juggle Letters 1

1. LUTRBDE = 1. _____
   Said

2. ERILKPY = 2. _____
   In a lively way

3. EFSOILB = 3. _____
   Minor weaknesses or failings of character

4. TEUM = 4. _____
   Silent; unable to speak

5. GEOOYLG = 5. _____
   Science of the origin, history and structure of the earth

6. EALNIODLM = 6. _____
   A large medal

7. AVNIE = 7. _____
   Simple; lacking in worldliness and sophistication

8. MSGIIUTTALN = 8. _____
   Exciting

9. ORPUTS = 9. _____
   Daze

10. TPEIFYR = 10. _____
    Come to become stonelike; to deaden

11. DNITINEG = 11. _____
    Impoverished; needy

12. NICBSANETE = 12. _____
    Deliberate restraining of oneself; not indulging

13. IEACMERD = 13. _____
    Government program for medical care for those over 65

14. DMIREMEZES = 14. _____
    Hypnotized

15. YESTASC = 15. _____
    Delight

Pigman's Legacy Vocabulary Juggle Letters 1 Answer Key

1. LUTRBDE = 1. BLURTED
   Said

2. ERILKPY = 2. PERKILY
   In a lively way

3. EFSOILB = 3. FOIBLES
   Minor weaknesses or failings of character

4. TEUM = 4. MUTE
   Silent; unable to speak

5. GEOOYLG = 5. GEOLOGY
   Science of the origin, history and structure of the earth

6. EALNIODLM = 6. MEDALLION
   A large medal

7. AVNIE = 7. NAIVE
   Simple; lacking in worldliness and sophistication

8. MSGIIUTTALN = 8. STIMULATING
   Exciting

9. ORPUTS = 9. STUPOR
   Daze

10. TPEIFYR = 10. PETRIFY
    Come to become stonelike; to deaden

11. DNITINEG = 11. INDIGENT
    Impoverished; needy

12. NICBSANETE = 12. ABSTINENCE
    Deliberate restraining of oneself; not indulging

13. IEACMERD = 13. MEDICARE
    Government program for medical care for those over 65

14. DMIREMEZES = 14. MESMERIZED
    Hypnotized

15. YESTASC = 15. ECSTASY
    Delight

Pigman's Legacy Vocabulary Juggle Letters 2

1. USOARUTSSGE = 1. _____
   Dinosaur with a double row of bony plates on its back

2. IWWOD = 2. _____
   Woman whose husband has died

3. TAMUNTLIISG = 3. _____
   Exciting

4. INHGUAS = 4. _____
   Agonizing physical or mental pain

5. DNNCOEO = 5. _____
   Overlook; forgive; disregard

6. YCGEAL = 6. _____
   Something handed down, as from an ancestor

7. AGRENDEV = 7. _____
   Carved or etched into a surface

8. EBULDTR = 8. _____
   Said

9. DMERSEMEIZ = 9. _____
   Hypnotized

10. PEIC = 10. _____
    Literary work that suggests grandeur or heroics

11. ISSFOL = 11. _____
    Skeleton or leaf imprint

12. SYSAETC = 12. _____
    Delight

13. IVOINS = 13. _____
    Experience of seeing the supernatural as if with the eyes

14. ETVNEDIR = 14. _____
    Turned inside out or up and down

15. ETRRESG = 15. _____
    Feels sorry about

Pigman's Legacy Vocabulary Juggle Letters 2 Answer Key

1. USOARUTSSGE = 1. STEGOSAURUS
Dinosaur with a double row of bony plates on its back

2. IWWOD = 2. WIDOW
Woman whose husband has died

3. TAMUNTLIISG = 3. STIMULATING
Exciting

4. INHGUAS = 4. ANGUISH
Agonizing physical or mental pain

5. DNNCOEO = 5. CONDONE
Overlook; forgive; disregard

6. YCGEAL = 6. LEGACY
Something handed down, as from an ancestor

7. AGRENDEV = 7. ENGRAVED
Carved or etched into a surface

8. EBULDTR = 8. BLURTED
Said

9. DMERSEMEIZ = 9. MESMERIZED
Hypnotized

10. PEIC =10. EPIC
Literary work that suggests grandeur or heroics

11. ISSFOL =11. FOSSIL
Skeleton or leaf imprint

12. SYSAETC =12. ECSTASY
Delight

13. IVOINS =13. VISION
Experience of seeing the supernatural as if with the eyes

14. ETVNEDIR =14. INVERTED
Turned inside out or up and down

15. ETRRESG =15. REGRETS
Feels sorry about

Pigman's Legacy Vocabulary Juggle Letters 3

1. YOPYOGLCHS = 1. _____
   Science that deals with mental processes and behavior

2. NICVCOOITN = 2. _____
   Strong belief

3. VCNUSVEAISISO = 3. _____
   Liveliness; spiritedness; animation

4. EEEMRZISMD = 4. _____
   Hypnotized

5. NEIRRESEFI = 5. _____
   Plants that purify crude substances

6. EAVNI = 6. _____
   Simple; lacking in worldliness and sophistication

7. IEFLENGC = 7. _____
   Defrauding of money or property; swindling

8. OROTSIHMBS = 8. _____
   Formation of blood clot in a vessel or the heart

9. IIOTNLITSAM = 9. _____
   Restrictions; boundaries

10. EPRLYKI = 10. _____
    In a lively way

11. REBUSEMDG = 11. _____
    Under; beneath

12. ALMMIEOR = 12. _____
    Commemorating, serving as a reminder of

13. LDBRETU = 13. _____
    Said

14. HAGIUNS = 14. _____
    Agonizing physical or mental pain

15. MZIEBOS = 15. _____
    People who look and behave like robots

Pigman's Legacy Vocabulary Juggle Letters 3 Answer Key

1. YOPYOGLCHS = 1. PSYCHOLOGY
   Science that deals with mental processes and behavior
2. NICVCOOITN = 2. CONVICTION
   Strong belief
3. VCNUSVEAISISO = 3. VIVACIOUSNESS
   Liveliness; spiritedness; animation
4. EEEMRZISMD = 4. MESMERIZED
   Hypnotized
5. NEIRRESEFI = 5. REFINERIES
   Plants that purify crude substances
6. EAVNI = 6. NAIVE
   Simple; lacking in worldliness and sophistication
7. IEFLENGC = 7. FLEECING
   Defrauding of money or property; swindling
8. OROTSIHMBS = 8. THROMBOSIS
   Formation of blood clot in a vessel or the heart
9. IIOTNLITSAM = 9. LIMITATIONS
   Restrictions; boundaries
10. EPRLYKI =10. PERKILY
    In a lively way
11. REBUSEMDG =11. SUBMERGED
    Under; beneath
12. ALMMIEOR =12. MEMORIAL
    Commemorating, serving as a reminder of
13. LDBRETU =13. BLURTED
    Said
14. HAGIUNS =14. ANGUISH
    Agonizing physical or mental pain
15. MZIEBOS =15. ZOMBIES
    People who look and behave like robots

Pigman's Legacy Vocabulary Juggle Letters 4

1. IAOYPLLNALTC = 1. _____
   Transcending physical desire; spiritual

2. SLISOF = 2. _____
   Skeleton or leaf imprint

3. FGRFU = 3. _____
   Brief and unfriendly; harsh

4. POTUSR = 4. _____
   Daze

5. ENIRVETD = 5. _____
   Turned inside out or up and down

6. DMRUEGESB = 6. _____
   Under; beneath

7. AMOIEMLR = 7. _____
   Commemorating, serving as a reminder of

8. UITULANDNG = 8. _____
   Making a wavelike movement

9. GFEINELC = 9. _____
   Defrauding of money or property; swindling

10. TONCCIVINO =10. _____
    Strong belief

11. SRTMISHOOB =11. _____
    Formation of blood clot in a vessel or the heart

12. OIFSLBE =12. _____
    Minor weaknesses or failings of character

13. EHZEEW =13. _____
    Hoarse whistling sound

14. ISEDILPC =14. _____
    Assistant; follower

15. TNOECVN =15. _____
    A monastic community or house, especially of nuns

Pigman's Legacy Vocabulary Juggle Letters 4 Answer Key

1. IAOYPLLNALTC = 1. PLATONICALLY
   Transcending physical desire; spiritual

2. SLISOF = 2. FOSSIL
   Skeleton or leaf imprint

3. FGRFU = 3. GRUFF
   Brief and unfriendly; harsh

4. POTUSR = 4. STUPOR
   Daze

5. ENIRVETD = 5. INVERTED
   Turned inside out or up and down

6. DMRUEGESB = 6. SUBMERGED
   Under; beneath

7. AMOIEMLR = 7. MEMORIAL
   Commemorating, serving as a reminder of

8. UITULANDNG = 8. UNDULATING
   Making a wavelike movement

9. GFEINELC = 9. FLEECING
   Defrauding of money or property; swindling

10. TONCCIVINO = 10. CONVICTION
    Strong belief

11. SRTMISHOOB = 11. THROMBOSIS
    Formation of blood clot in a vessel or the heart

12. OIFSLBE = 12. FOIBLES
    Minor weaknesses or failings of character

13. EHZEEW = 13. WHEEZE
    Hoarse whistling sound

14. ISEDILPC = 14. DISCIPLE
    Assistant; follower

15. TNOECVN = 15. CONVENT
    A monastic community or house, especially of nuns

ABSTINENCE	Deliberate restraining of oneself; not indulging
ADOLESCENCE	Period from puberty to maturity; teen years
ANGUISH	Agonizing physical or mental pain
APPARITION	A ghost
BLURTED	Said
CONDONE	Overlook; forgive; disregard

CONVENT	A monastic community or house, especially of nuns
CONVICTION	Strong belief
DILAPIDATED	In disrepair, deterioration, or ruin
DISCIPLE	Assistant; follower
DOSSIER	Collection of papers about a particular person
ECSTASY	Delight

ENGRAVED	Carved or etched into a surface
EPIC	Literary work that suggests grandeur or heroics
FLEECING	Defrauding of money or property; swindling
FOIBLES	Minor weaknesses or failings of character
FOSSIL	Skeleton or leaf imprint
FRAIL	Not substantial; slight

GEOLOGY	Science of the origin, history and structure of the earth
GRAFFITI	Drawing or inscription on wall or other surface
GRUFF	Brief and unfriendly; harsh
IGNITED	Lit up
IMMERSE	Cover completely in something else
INDIGENT	Impoverished; needy

INSTINCTIVE	Impulsive
INVERTED	Turned inside out or up and down
KEOGH	Retirement plan for the self-employed
LEGACY	Something handed down, as from an ancestor
LIMITATIONS	Restrictions; boundaries
MANNEQUINS	Dummies

MAUSOLEUM	A large stately tomb
MEDALLION	A large medal
MEDICARE	Government program for medical care for those over 65
MEMORIAL	Commemorating, serving as a reminder of
MESMERIZED	Hypnotized
MORTIFIED	Humiliated; shamed

MUTE	Silent; unable to speak
NAIVE	Simple; lacking in worldliness and sophistication
OMEN	Sigh of future good or evil
PERKILY	In a lively way
PETRIFY	Come to become stonelike; to deaden
PLATONICALLY	Transcending physical desire; spiritual

PSYCHOLOGY	Science that deals with mental processes and behavior
PUBESCENT	Reaching or having reached puberty
REFINERIES	Plants that purify crude substances
REGRETS	Feels sorry about
REINCARNATED	Reborn
REVERIE	A state of abstract musing

RHINESTONE	A colorless artificial gem of paste or glass
SERENDIPITY	Ability to make fortunate discoveries by accident
SHRINE	Site revered for its associations
SQUATTING	Settling without legal claim
STEGOSAURUS	Dinosaur with a double row of bony plates on its back
STIMULATING	Exciting

STUPOR	Daze
SUBMERGED	Under; beneath
SURREPTITIOUSLY	Secretly
THROMBOSIS	Formation of blood clot in a vessel or the heart
TRESPASSING	Invading the property rights of another
UNDULATING	Making a wavelike movement

VISION	Experience of seeing the supernatural as if with the eyes
VIVACIOUSNESS	Liveliness; spiritedness; animation
WHEEZE	Hoarse whistling sound
WIDOW	Woman whose husband has died
ZOMBIES	People who look and behave like robots

Pigman's Legacy Vocabulary

STEGOSAURUS	SQUATTING	LEGACY	NAIVE	WIDOW
INVERTED	MANNEQUINS	STIMULATING	MAUSOLEUM	FLEECING
STUPOR	MEDICARE	FREE SPACE	THROMBOSIS	PSYCHOLOGY
UNDULATING	ANGUISH	IGNITED	APPARITION	KEOGH
CONVICTION	ECSTASY	ABSTINENCE	TRESPASSING	GRAFFITI

Pigman's Legacy Vocabulary

VISION	ADOLESCENCE	RHINESTONE	REGRETS	CONVENT
IMMERSE	MORTIFIED	EPIC	SHRINE	FOIBLES
SERENDIPITY	WHEEZE	FREE SPACE	REVERIE	ZOMBIES
REINCARNATED	DILAPIDATED	PETRIFY	REFINERIES	DOSSIER
FRAIL	PLATONICALLY	MEDALLION	LIMITATIONS	BLURTED

Pigman's Legacy Vocabulary

REINCARNATED	EPIC	ENGRAVED	BLURTED	ECSTASY
SERENDIPITY	FOIBLES	TRESPASSING	SUBMERGED	REFINERIES
PLATONICALLY	CONVICTION	FREE SPACE	VIVACIOUSNESS	FLEECING
DILAPIDATED	NAIVE	MORTIFIED	DOSSIER	THROMBOSIS
MAUSOLEUM	VISION	PUBESCENT	APPARITION	REVERIE

Pigman's Legacy Vocabulary

MANNEQUINS	ZOMBIES	MEMORIAL	INDIGENT	MESMERIZED
MUTE	UNDULATING	SQUATTING	KEOGH	STUPOR
GRAFFITI	WHEEZE	FREE SPACE	SHRINE	CONVENT
INSTINCTIVE	IGNITED	REGRETS	FRAIL	STEGOSAURUS
FOSSIL	DISCIPLE	LIMITATIONS	IMMERSE	MEDICARE

Pigman's Legacy Vocabulary

GRUFF	REFINERIES	INVERTED	CONVENT	REVERIE
MUTE	ADOLESCENCE	PLATONICALLY	OMEN	MANNEQUINS
STUPOR	PUBESCENT	FREE SPACE	MEMORIAL	BLURTED
SUBMERGED	GEOLOGY	DOSSIER	DILAPIDATED	ZOMBIES
ANGUISH	CONVICTION	MESMERIZED	CONDONE	APPARITION

Pigman's Legacy Vocabulary

INDIGENT	MORTIFIED	MAUSOLEUM	SHRINE	NAIVE
TRESPASSING	SERENDIPITY	EPIC	SURREPTITIOUSLY	INSTINCTIVE
IMMERSE	ABSTINENCE	FREE SPACE	FLEECING	SQUATTING
VISION	MEDALLION	STEGOSAURUS	VIVACIOUSNESS	WIDOW
PERKILY	PSYCHOLOGY	REGRETS	UNDULATING	KEOGH

Pigman's Legacy Vocabulary

MESMERIZED	BLURTED	WIDOW	PUBESCENT	IMMERSE
ABSTINENCE	SQUATTING	WHEEZE	FLEECING	THROMBOSIS
FOSSIL	TRESPASSING	FREE SPACE	CONVENT	MUTE
ENGRAVED	LEGACY	NAIVE	MEMORIAL	CONDONE
FRAIL	REINCARNATED	STUPOR	MORTIFIED	CONVICTION

Pigman's Legacy Vocabulary

UNDULATING	OMEN	MEDICARE	GRAFFITI	EPIC
DILAPIDATED	GRUFF	KEOGH	VISION	IGNITED
VIVACIOUSNESS	INVERTED	FREE SPACE	MAUSOLEUM	SUBMERGED
DOSSIER	STIMULATING	RHINESTONE	REVERIE	GEOLOGY
STEGOSAURUS	PERKILY	MANNEQUINS	REGRETS	PLATONICALLY

Pigman's Legacy Vocabulary

REVERIE	VISION	CONDONE	NAIVE	REGRETS
INSTINCTIVE	LIMITATIONS	ECSTASY	CONVENT	SQUATTING
INDIGENT	OMEN	FREE SPACE	MORTIFIED	MEDICARE
SURREPTITIOUSLY	REINCARNATED	RHINESTONE	FLEECING	WHEEZE
INVERTED	VIVACIOUSNESS	DOSSIER	WIDOW	TRESPASSING

Pigman's Legacy Vocabulary

MEMORIAL	FOSSIL	DILAPIDATED	FRAIL	KEOGH
EPIC	GRAFFITI	PUBESCENT	ENGRAVED	ADOLESCENCE
UNDULATING	MANNEQUINS	FREE SPACE	PLATONICALLY	CONVICTION
FOIBLES	GEOLOGY	BLURTED	SUBMERGED	MAUSOLEUM
STIMULATING	IGNITED	IMMERSE	GRUFF	STEGOSAURUS

Pigman's Legacy Vocabulary

ADOLESCENCE	CONVICTION	INDIGENT	DOSSIER	NAIVE
DISCIPLE	MEDICARE	REVERIE	FLEECING	MEMORIAL
INVERTED	SQUATTING	FREE SPACE	IGNITED	ANGUISH
SHRINE	WHEEZE	MORTIFIED	APPARITION	INSTINCTIVE
MANNEQUINS	FOSSIL	BLURTED	REFINERIES	LIMITATIONS

Pigman's Legacy Vocabulary

STEGOSAURUS	MESMERIZED	WIDOW	FOIBLES	ZOMBIES
THROMBOSIS	VIVACIOUSNESS	GEOLOGY	SUBMERGED	PERKILY
EPIC	VISION	FREE SPACE	UNDULATING	SURREPTITIOUSLY
CONVENT	STIMULATING	PSYCHOLOGY	GRAFFITI	LEGACY
PUBESCENT	STUPOR	FRAIL	ECSTASY	ENGRAVED

Pigman's Legacy Vocabulary

STEGOSAURUS	DILAPIDATED	DOSSIER	MAUSOLEUM	BLURTED
APPARITION	WIDOW	ADOLESCENCE	SERENDIPITY	INVERTED
PSYCHOLOGY	RHINESTONE	FREE SPACE	GEOLOGY	ENGRAVED
CONDONE	REGRETS	MESMERIZED	INDIGENT	EPIC
PETRIFY	VISION	PERKILY	INSTINCTIVE	REFINERIES

Pigman's Legacy Vocabulary

IGNITED	LEGACY	VIVACIOUSNESS	MORTIFIED	SQUATTING
LIMITATIONS	DISCIPLE	ANGUISH	GRUFF	IMMERSE
ECSTASY	ZOMBIES	FREE SPACE	CONVENT	MUTE
MANNEQUINS	NAIVE	MEMORIAL	PUBESCENT	FRAIL
SUBMERGED	FOSSIL	SURREPTITIOUSLY	ABSTINENCE	REINCARNATED

Pigman's Legacy Vocabulary

EPIC	MAUSOLEUM	ECSTASY	REFINERIES	GEOLOGY
THROMBOSIS	MESMERIZED	FRAIL	FOIBLES	CONVICTION
VISION	OMEN	FREE SPACE	PETRIFY	INSTINCTIVE
RHINESTONE	SURREPTITIOUSLY	STEGOSAURUS	PERKILY	INVERTED
TRESPASSING	FLEECING	LEGACY	MEDALLION	SUBMERGED

Pigman's Legacy Vocabulary

BLURTED	REINCARNATED	DILAPIDATED	MEMORIAL	PSYCHOLOGY
PLATONICALLY	WHEEZE	MEDICARE	CONVENT	FOSSIL
IGNITED	LIMITATIONS	FREE SPACE	GRUFF	SHRINE
ZOMBIES	VIVACIOUSNESS	WIDOW	MUTE	STUPOR
KEOGH	STIMULATING	DOSSIER	ADOLESCENCE	GRAFFITI

Pigman's Legacy Vocabulary

UNDULATING	REVERIE	VIVACIOUSNESS	ADOLESCENCE	SHRINE
ECSTASY	MEDALLION	SQUATTING	PSYCHOLOGY	REFINERIES
WHEEZE	STIMULATING	FREE SPACE	GEOLOGY	THROMBOSIS
GRUFF	MEMORIAL	IGNITED	ABSTINENCE	MORTIFIED
SUBMERGED	MANNEQUINS	RHINESTONE	NAIVE	LEGACY

Pigman's Legacy Vocabulary

PERKILY	BLURTED	DISCIPLE	CONVICTION	INVERTED
FOIBLES	SURREPTITIOUSLY	MEDICARE	CONVENT	KEOGH
MESMERIZED	EPIC	FREE SPACE	INDIGENT	STEGOSAURUS
DILAPIDATED	MUTE	PETRIFY	OMEN	GRAFFITI
ENGRAVED	IMMERSE	APPARITION	INSTINCTIVE	TRESPASSING

Pigman's Legacy Vocabulary

MUTE	CONDONE	FOSSIL	MEDICARE	IMMERSE
VISION	MESMERIZED	GRUFF	MAUSOLEUM	WIDOW
PETRIFY	KEOGH	FREE SPACE	RHINESTONE	SURREPTITIOUSLY
REFINERIES	REVERIE	ADOLESCENCE	ABSTINENCE	SUBMERGED
CONVICTION	INVERTED	ECSTASY	FRAIL	EPIC

Pigman's Legacy Vocabulary

PSYCHOLOGY	BLURTED	SHRINE	SQUATTING	STEGOSAURUS
OMEN	THROMBOSIS	DISCIPLE	VIVACIOUSNESS	UNDULATING
PLATONICALLY	IGNITED	FREE SPACE	WHEEZE	GEOLOGY
CONVENT	STIMULATING	NAIVE	PUBESCENT	ENGRAVED
MORTIFIED	MEDALLION	INSTINCTIVE	PERKILY	DOSSIER

Pigman's Legacy Vocabulary

KEOGH	INSTINCTIVE	DISCIPLE	SERENDIPITY	PERKILY
MEDALLION	PLATONICALLY	NAIVE	PETRIFY	STIMULATING
EPIC	THROMBOSIS	FREE SPACE	VIVACIOUSNESS	SUBMERGED
FRAIL	REVERIE	INDIGENT	ANGUISH	ENGRAVED
MEDICARE	GEOLOGY	LEGACY	MEMORIAL	VISION

Pigman's Legacy Vocabulary

DOSSIER	APPARITION	MORTIFIED	BLURTED	SURREPTITIOUSLY
RHINESTONE	MUTE	REGRETS	MAUSOLEUM	REFINERIES
DILAPIDATED	INVERTED	FREE SPACE	ZOMBIES	LIMITATIONS
GRUFF	FOIBLES	FOSSIL	SQUATTING	TRESPASSING
IGNITED	MESMERIZED	UNDULATING	ECSTASY	STEGOSAURUS

Pigman's Legacy Vocabulary

DISCIPLE	SERENDIPITY	REVERIE	OMEN	SURREPTITIOUSLY
MESMERIZED	INVERTED	ZOMBIES	PUBESCENT	ENGRAVED
UNDULATING	MEDALLION	FREE SPACE	WHEEZE	BLURTED
KEOGH	RHINESTONE	INSTINCTIVE	MUTE	APPARITION
REFINERIES	PLATONICALLY	VISION	MAUSOLEUM	MANNEQUINS

Pigman's Legacy Vocabulary

CONDONE	MEDICARE	ADOLESCENCE	INDIGENT	STIMULATING
GRAFFITI	DILAPIDATED	GEOLOGY	THROMBOSIS	STEGOSAURUS
PSYCHOLOGY	FRAIL	FREE SPACE	SHRINE	DOSSIER
SQUATTING	WIDOW	LEGACY	ANGUISH	ECSTASY
EPIC	MEMORIAL	GRUFF	FOSSIL	TRESPASSING

Pigman's Legacy Vocabulary

PERKILY	STIMULATING	MANNEQUINS	INVERTED	ECSTASY
SERENDIPITY	PSYCHOLOGY	REINCARNATED	MORTIFIED	GEOLOGY
CONVENT	UNDULATING	FREE SPACE	ZOMBIES	FRAIL
GRUFF	WIDOW	FOIBLES	INDIGENT	LIMITATIONS
REFINERIES	CONDONE	PLATONICALLY	LEGACY	WHEEZE

Pigman's Legacy Vocabulary

VISION	EPIC	PUBESCENT	SUBMERGED	REGRETS
ADOLESCENCE	ENGRAVED	DOSSIER	APPARITION	ANGUISH
MUTE	INSTINCTIVE	FREE SPACE	SQUATTING	MEMORIAL
NAIVE	SHRINE	KEOGH	OMEN	MEDICARE
ABSTINENCE	MAUSOLEUM	THROMBOSIS	PETRIFY	GRAFFITI

Pigman's Legacy Vocabulary

IGNITED	RHINESTONE	PERKILY	REINCARNATED	VISION
ZOMBIES	FOSSIL	APPARITION	DILAPIDATED	FOIBLES
LIMITATIONS	CONVICTION	FREE SPACE	FLEECING	PLATONICALLY
WHEEZE	ANGUISH	GRAFFITI	MUTE	BLURTED
MANNEQUINS	THROMBOSIS	SQUATTING	FRAIL	REGRETS

Pigman's Legacy Vocabulary

CONDONE	OMEN	ADOLESCENCE	EPIC	SUBMERGED
REFINERIES	MEDICARE	CONVENT	MEDALLION	NAIVE
TRESPASSING	MEMORIAL	FREE SPACE	GRUFF	PETRIFY
STUPOR	GEOLOGY	STIMULATING	INVERTED	IMMERSE
DOSSIER	ECSTASY	STEGOSAURUS	ABSTINENCE	UNDULATING

Pigman's Legacy Vocabulary

INDIGENT	SQUATTING	MEMORIAL	MANNEQUINS	GRAFFITI
PUBESCENT	APPARITION	RHINESTONE	IGNITED	UNDULATING
DILAPIDATED	BLURTED	FREE SPACE	VISION	MEDICARE
NAIVE	DISCIPLE	PSYCHOLOGY	ENGRAVED	IMMERSE
PERKILY	FOSSIL	SURREPTITIOUSLY	MAUSOLEUM	SHRINE

Pigman's Legacy Vocabulary

KEOGH	EPIC	GEOLOGY	CONVICTION	TRESPASSING
MEDALLION	PETRIFY	SERENDIPITY	THROMBOSIS	FOIBLES
STUPOR	INSTINCTIVE	FREE SPACE	WIDOW	STIMULATING
MORTIFIED	CONVENT	OMEN	REGRETS	VIVACIOUSNESS
ABSTINENCE	DOSSIER	MESMERIZED	ANGUISH	STEGOSAURUS

Pigman's Legacy Vocabulary

IGNITED	FRAIL	ADOLESCENCE	GRAFFITI	IMMERSE
REFINERIES	INDIGENT	CONVENT	MAUSOLEUM	ANGUISH
FLEECING	STEGOSAURUS	FREE SPACE	DISCIPLE	WHEEZE
NAIVE	SUBMERGED	SHRINE	EPIC	REVERIE
UNDULATING	MESMERIZED	PETRIFY	PLATONICALLY	MEDALLION

Pigman's Legacy Vocabulary

VISION	CONVICTION	SQUATTING	REGRETS	APPARITION
MUTE	MORTIFIED	INSTINCTIVE	MEDICARE	FOIBLES
GRUFF	MANNEQUINS	FREE SPACE	DOSSIER	ECSTASY
INVERTED	RHINESTONE	ABSTINENCE	THROMBOSIS	LEGACY
VIVACIOUSNESS	FOSSIL	LIMITATIONS	PUBESCENT	TRESPASSING